AFTA SpringerBriefs in Family Therapy

A Publication of the American Family Therapy Academy

Founded in 1977, the **American Family Therapy Academy** is a nonprofit organization of leading family therapy teachers, clinicians, program directors, policymakers, researchers, and social scientists dedicated to advancing systemic thinking and practices for families in their social context.

Vision

AFTA envisions a just world by transforming social contexts that promote health, safety, and well-being of all families and communities.

Mission

AFTA's mission is developing, researching, teaching, and disseminating progressive, just family therapy and family-centered practices and policies.

More information about this series at http://www.springer.com/series/11846

Elisabeth Esmiol Wilson • Lindsey Nice
Editors

Socially Just Religious and Spiritual Interventions

Ethical Uses of Therapeutic Power

AFTA
American Family Therapy Academy

Springer

Editors
Elisabeth Esmiol Wilson
Marriage and Family Therapy Program
Pacific Lutheran University
Tacoma, WA, USA

Lindsey Nice
Marriage and Family Therapy Program
Pacific Lutheran University
Tacoma, WA, USA

ISSN 2196-5528 ISSN 2196-5536 (electronic)
AFTA SpringerBriefs in Family Therapy
ISBN 978-3-030-01985-3 ISBN 978-3-030-01986-0 (eBook)
https://doi.org/10.1007/978-3-030-01986-0

Library of Congress Control Number: 2018960174

This Springer imprint is published by the registered company Springer Nature Switzerland AG
The registered company address is: Gewerbestrasse 11, 6330 Cham, Switzerland

Series Editor Foreword

The AFTA Springer Briefs in Family Therapy is an official publication of the American Family Therapy Academy. Each volume focuses on the practice and policy implications of innovative systemic research and theory in family therapy and allied fields. Our goal is to make information about families and systemic practices in societal contexts widely accessible in a reader-friendly, conversational, and practical style. AFTA's core commitments to equality, social responsibility, and justice are represented in each volume.

In *Socially Just Religious and Spiritual Interventions: Ethical Uses of Therapeutic Power*, editors Elisabeth Esmiol Wilson and Lindsey Nice asked chapter authors to take on a task that mental health professionals have typically avoided: to address the intersection of religion and spirituality with sociopolitical contexts and dominant discourses around issues such as race, gender, sexuality, and socioeconomic status in their clinical work. The book begins with a framework to guide the assessment of clients' spiritual/religious contexts along a spectrum from potentially harmful/oppressive to healing/empowering that can help open conversation about them. Readers are encouraged to consider the ethical implications of how they use their therapeutic power, inviting us to challenge possible societal inequities of clients' beliefs and practices while supporting and enhancing empowering ones.

Chapter authors share their rich knowledge and experience bridging social justice and spiritual/religious concerns on a range of complex and often heart-wrenching topics including Asian American Christianity, religious disaffiliation, mixed orientation marriage, transgender families, infertility, transracial adoption, parent-child attachment, affairs, and acute and chronic illness. While providing detailed, up-to-date information on these topics, the authors also capture the lived experience of people struggling with tensions inherent in their situations, often sharing their own personal experience. The book is a refreshing antidote to current sociopolitical and cultural divides. Each chapter shows that hope and connection across differences are not only possible; they heal.

Carmen Knudson-Martin
AFTA Springer Briefs in Family Therapy
Lewis & Clark College
Portland, OR, USA

Acknowledgments

The vision for this book and the development of the framework presented in Chap. 1 and utilized in each following chapter emerged during Elisabeth Esmiol Wilson's sabbatical. Carmen Knudson-Martin was invaluable in encouraging the initial framework, as well as supporting the idea for a collaborative volume. The volume grew in earnest as 14 authors with diverse backgrounds and clinical experiences joined the project and drew on the framework in their own specific areas of practice. As Elisabeth and Lindsey Nice partnered as coeditors, we processed through the many nuances of an ethical and socially justice approach to applying spiritual and religious interventions across multiple presenting issues. Each chapter represents the unique contributions of authors engaging and collaborating with the overarching ideas presented in Chap. 1 but applied specifically and creatively based on particular author expertise.

As coeditors and colleagues, teaching together in a master's level marriage and family therapy program, we are deeply indebted to the many faculty meeting tangents in which together with our department chair, David Ward, we passionately discussed, debated, disagreed, and always explored with respect the possible influences of specific religious beliefs (held by therapists or clients) on the practice of marriage and family therapy.

We also recognize the deep influence of our own particular experiences in various faith communities. We hold gratitude for both the joys and injuries we experienced within these communities and how the ability to hold both helped shape the direction of this work. In particular, Elisabeth's experience in seminary and subsequent years practicing as a spiritual director were invaluable in the development of Chap. 1's framework. I (Elisabeth) extend gratitude to each of my spiritual directees and especially to Nancy Duvall, my former seminary professor and long-time mentor and friend, whose deep relationality, spirituality, and ability to encourage embracing dichotomies as mysteries infuse this work.

Our work teaching in the classroom and supervising developing family therapists has both influenced and inspired this work. We are grateful for the ways in which our students have taught and challenged us. We are also indebted to the many voices in our larger family therapy field that spurred us to deeper levels of contextual, social justice-oriented, and inclusionary integration, in particular the writings of Carmen Knudson-Martin and AnaLouise Keating.

We are grateful to the American Family Therapy Academy, a professional home to both of us, and a community commitment to "challeng[ing] the institutional and interpersonal policies and practices as well as the underlying ideologies that perpetuate the continuation of these contemporary and historical injustices" (AFTA statement on social justice). We are grateful for the AFTA Springer Briefs in Family Therapy, for the support and collaboration of our mentor and now Series Editor, Carmen Knudson-Martin, and for Jennifer Hadley and the team at Springer Science. We also want to give a special thank you to Holly Harden, our student and administrative assistant, for her close editing, careful proofreading, checking, and rechecking. This team's ongoing belief and encouragement in the value and importance of this volume has been a huge support.

Without a sabbatical, this project would not have materialized. We thank Pacific Lutheran University for funding a sabbatical during which Elisabeth in particular devoted the time and energy to developing what is now the *justice-informed framework for spiritual and religious resilience*.

We are both grateful to our families for not only their support but for being the fabric in which we developed and continue to develop our own understanding of ourselves as spiritual beings. We are blessed to have partners with whom we can explore, question, and share spiritual meanings and navigate the sometimes beautiful, sometimes tragic impacts of faith and religion. Both Jeff and Aaron have been incredibly supportive and constant encouragers throughout this project.

Finally, we thank each of the authors who contributed to this volume. We asked you to share a part of your own journey and identity and write about the specifics of your clinical work in an engaging and applicable manner. We are moved and amazed by your voices and how particularly you each reflect a socially just stance in integrating spirituality and religion in your clinical work. Thank you for your individual and collective contribution to the field. We hope that others will be as inspired by your clinical wisdom as we are.

Elisabeth Esmiol Wilson
Lindsey Nice

Contents

Contributors

Jessica L. ChenFeng University Medical Center, Loma Linda University, Loma Linda, CA, USA

Elizabeth D'Arrigo-Patrick California State University, San Bernardino, CA, USA

Justine D'Arrigo-Patrick California State University, San Bernardino, CA, USA

Barbara Couden Hernandez Loma Linda University School of Medicine, Loma Linda, CA, USA

Chris Hoff California State University, San Bernardino, CA, USA

Lana Kim Department of Counseling Psychology, Lewis & Clark College, Portland, OR, USA

April Knight Private Marriage and Family Therapy Practice, Tacoma, WA, USA

Elijah C. Nealy Department of Social Work and Equitable Community Practice, University of Saint Joseph, West Hartford, CT, USA

Lindsey Nice Marriage and Family Therapy Program, Pacific Lutheran University, Tacoma, WA, USA

Lina S. Ponder Biola University, La Mirada, CA, USA

Brenda Rogers Rogers Family Counseling, Federal Way, WA, USA

Sarah K. Samman Couple and Family Therapy Program, Alliant University, San Diego campus, San Diego, CA, USA

Joshua Weed Private Marriage and Family Therapy Practice in Kent, Kent, WA, USA

Kirstee Williams Department of Behavioral and Social Sciences, Lee University, Cleveland, TN, USA

Elisabeth Esmiol Wilson Marriage and Family Therapy Program, Pacific Lutheran University, Tacoma, WA, USA

Editors

Elisabeth Esmiol Wilson PhD, LMFT, is an Associate Professor and Director of Clinical Training at Pacific Lutheran University. She has an MA in Spiritual Formation and Soul Care and practiced as a spiritual director before becoming a family therapist. Her research focuses on couples' experiences of gender, power, and spirituality and on clinical training issues including attending to larger contextual issues and integrating client feedback into treatment. She enjoys running an active private practice focusing on sexual and spiritual issues in couple therapy and continues to practice as a spiritual director.

Lindsey Nice PhD, LMFT, RN, is an Assistant Professor and Clinic Director at Pacific Lutheran University in Tacoma, WA. Before becoming an MFT, she worked as a nurse at a small hospital in OR and still enjoys learning about the intersection of physical, mental, and relational health. Her research interests include medical family therapy, religion and spirituality in therapy, MFT pedagogy, experiential teaching interventions, and relational equality. In her free time, she enjoys working on the 1930's farm she and her husband are renovating.

Chapter 1
From Assessment to Activism: Utilizing a Justice-Informed Framework to Guide Spiritual and Religious Clinical Interventions

Elisabeth Esmiol Wilson

On Seeing Rightly
I stepped outside
Blinking in the bright summer sun
My bare feet on the warm wooden deck.
My eyes adjusting, I blinked
Then gasped, and stared.
Massive white blossoms
Each larger than my fist
Covered a dark green plant
Nearly two stories tall.
Perhaps an overgrown bush or hedge
Entirely more white than green
Grew like an explosion of light,
The blossoms seeming to glow
Emitting their sweet smell
In that burning summer sun.
I stood transfixed not expecting
To be so ravished
By beauty,
My breath taken away
By such overwhelming radiance,
Nothing subtle or demure
But grabbing my attention
Filling my line of vision
Boldly captivating my senses:
The light, the white
The sweet warm fragrance.
And in my awed silence
I heard You whisper
"That is how I see you."

E. Esmiol Wilson (✉)
Marriage and Family Therapy Program, Pacific Lutheran University, Tacoma, WA, USA
e-mail: esmiolev@plu.edu

E. Esmiol Wilson, L. Nice (eds.), *Socially Just Religious and Spiritual Interventions*,
AFTA SpringerBriefs in Family Therapy, https://doi.org/10.1007/978-3-030-01986-0_1

I wrote this poem while working with a deeply religious female client who was struggling to see her own beauty and worth. As we worked through early childhood abandonment, sexual abuse, and relational cutoffs, her Catholic faith and specifically her relationship with Mary remained the strongest attachment in her life. Together we countered rigid beliefs about herself, such as "I disobeyed God and now I can never live out my true calling," with other more helpful religious beliefs she held, such as "I know 'the steadfast love of the Lord never ceases, his mercies never come to an end, they are new every morning'" (Lamentations 3:22, NRSVCE). Slowly my client began to see herself differently through God's eyes, experiencing herself as loved and valuable. While I have not yet shared this poem with my client, to me the words evoke a metaphor of her and other clients' spiritual and religious journeys into more wholeness.

For over 7 years, I have sat behind a one-way mirror watching my marriage and family therapy (MFT) graduate students tentatively engage in therapeutic conversations about spirituality and religion with their clients. In supervision, we discuss spiritually integrated interventions such as asking a recently unemployed Jehovah Witness man, "how might your faith foster hope for your future?" or a Muslim woman struggling with her divorce, "what religious practices might support your sense of self-worth?" When the topic of religion emerges, our conversations quickly become personal, whether overtly or not. I teach in the Pacific Northwest at a progressive Lutheran university in a graduate program that attracts students from a wide and often divergent spectrum of beliefs, sometimes in the process of being formed or unformed.

My own faith has undergone many permutations and revisions. While I was raised in the Episcopal Church and identify as a progressive Christian today, the churches I've chronologically attended as an adult, on both the East and West coasts, have exposed me to very disparate theologies: mainline Presbyterian and Congregational churches, two charismatic Vineyard churches, fundamental Baptist and nondenominational Evangelical churches, and a progressive LGBTQ-affirming Methodist church. I came to the MFT field via a theologically conservative seminary degree in spiritual formation and soul care, and I have seen the integration of spirituality and religion in my clinical work, and supervision reflects my own faith progression, in sometimes problematic ways (e.g., both over- and underemphasizing the importance of religion in a client's life). Critical reflection on my own works over time, and a commitment to training my students from their very diverse religious and nonreligious identities has made me fascinated with the ethics of how we clinically address religion and spiritually with our clients. Out of my interest in this sometimes-messy intersection between the self of the clinician's religious, spiritual, and/or moral meaning making, and the clinician's ability to critically self-reflect during therapeutic religious or spiritual interventions, emerged an ethical framework for practice.

In this chapter I will explore the positive and negative impacts of religion and spirituality on mental health and some of the contextual, training, and personal challenges of integrating spiritual/religious interventions in practice. I will highlight the need for a post-oppositional, ethical guideline and introduce the *justice-informed framework for spiritual and religious resilience*. Finally, I will illustrate the framework through a supervision case in which I supported two clinicians working together with an LDS wife and mother who had been diagnosed with terminal cancer and was afraid to die.

Impact of Religion and Spirituality on Mental Health and Relationships

Definitions and Distinctions

While sometimes cumbersome, I intentionally refer to both religion and spirituality because each term helps me capture something specific and different. Religion refers to a group's legitimized views on religious practices, often codified in religious texts, doctrines, etc. (Slater, Hall, & Edwards, 2003). Extrinsic religion tends to be utilitarian, where religion is a means to an end and holds a personal or social benefit (Hughes & Dickson, 2005). Intrinsic religion in contrast centers on religious commitment, a sense of meaning in life, and more internally motivated moral beliefs (Kirkpatrick & Hood, 1990). While helpful in understanding religious beliefs and practices, these extrinsic and intrinsic dimensions have been increasingly critiqued as poor measures of interaction with God (Hill & Hood, 1999; Kirkpatrick & Hood, 1990). Spirituality refers to this important dimension of the human-divine connection (Hall & Fujikawa, 2013). Spirituality includes a belief in something bigger than oneself, the search for something sacred, and focuses on how people relate to and experience the divine (Giblin, 2004; Hall & Fujikawa, 2013; Slater et al., 2003).

Positive and Negative Impacts on Mental Health

Recent decades have seen a growing body of research pointing to the importance of religion and spirituality on aiding mental health (George, Larsons, Koeing, & McCullough, 2000). Both religion and spirituality have the capacity to be incredibly powerful resources for clients (Pargament, 2007; Walsh, 2009). Weber and Pargament's (2014) review of the literature demonstrates that religion and spirituality have the capacity to promote mental health. Specifically, religion and spirituality can promote mental health through *positive religious coping*, such as praying for strength and support, *positive beliefs* such as "God loves me," and *positive community and support*, such as feeling a sense of belonging when attending a temple, a mass, or a mosque (Weber & Pargament, 2014). Additionally, for both religious and nonreligious, a stronger conviction in beliefs is correlated with more positive mental health (Baker & Cruickshank, 2010).

In contrast, and sometimes simultaneously, religion and spirituality can damage mental health and create incredibly significant and substantial difficulties for clients (Pargament, 2007). This occurs specifically through *negative religious coping*, such as feeling abandoned by God; *negative beliefs*, such as "God is angry and disappointed in me"; and *misunderstandings and miscommunication*, for example, feeling alienated by one's religious community (Weber & Pargament, 2014). Religion and spirituality can also negatively impact nonbelievers' mental health, as they are often more negatively perceived than believers and may be angry toward and less forgiving of God (Weber, Pargament, Kunik, Lomax, & Stanley, 2012).

Positive and Negative Impacts on Couple and Family Relationships

Additionally, family therapy research increasingly indicates that religion and spirituality can both positively and negatively influence couple and family relationships (Cattich & Knudson-Martin, 2009; Esmiol Wilson, Knudson-Martin, & Wilson, 2014; Giblin, 2004). For example, couples who engage in more mutual, relational patterns of connection seem to describe more empowering and relational connections with the divine (Cattich & Knudson-Martin, 2009; Esmiol Wilson et al. 2014). The same studies show that in contrast, power-imbalanced couples lacking in mutuality seem more likely to struggle with both spiritual coping and couple problem solving. While the direction of influence is unclear, the impact of couple connection on relationship with God, and relationship with God on couple connection, is likely reciprocal in nature and can likely evolve over time in increasingly helpful or damaging patterns of interaction (Cattich & Knudson-Martin, 2009).

Religion and Spirituality in Context

Larger Societal Discourses

The intersection of religion and spirituality with social discourses surrounding politics, race and ethnicity, and socioeconomic status intimately impacts our clinical work. Within the same month, I presented the *justice-informed framework for spiritual and religious resilience* to roughly 90 mental health clinicians in the Pacific Northwest (PNW) and then online to a consortium of mental health clinicians in Nairobi, Kenya. These differing contexts had a profound impact on the ethical challenges the clinicians faced. While Christianity is the dominant discourse in both countries, the PNW has the highest number of unchurched folks in the USA and had recently become the tenth US state to declare conversion therapy with clients under 18 unprofessional conducts. In contrast, same-sex marriage is still illegal in

Kenya, forced anal exams have only recently become illegal (Bhalla, 2018), and tribal tensions prevail in ethnocentric politics. We cannot separate our clinical practices from the complex influences of our immediate and larger societal discourses.

Challenges in Clinical Training and Practice

While historically clinical training programs were largely silent on issues of religion and spirituality, today core competencies across all major mental health fields regularly address religion and spirituality as important contextual issues, along with gender, race, ethnicity, sexual orientation, etc. (Weiler, Lyness, Haddock, & Zimmerman, 2015). With increased research on religion and spirituality also came the recognition that family therapy programs lacked robust training in using spirituality and religion as a clinical resource (Marterella & Brock, 2008; McNeil, Pavkov, Hecker, & Killmer, 2012; Walsh, 2009). A wave of research and clinical recommendations followed on how to integrate (Coyle, 2017) and measure (Carlson, McGeorge, & Toomey, 2014) spirituality training in family therapy programs. Yet the negative impact of such spirituality training on student practices such as working with LGBTQ clients has also been noticed (McGeorge, Carlson, & Toomey, 2014).

Consistent training in spiritual and religious interventions is further heightened by polarization across a spectrum of training programs. More religious (Christian) programs with strong faith-based missions tend to emphasize positive impacts of religion, yet we lack clear integration of clinical theory with religious world views (Walsh, 2009). Non-affiliated and loosely religiously affiliated programs tend to address religion as a contextual factor, yet typically lack rigorous training in assessment and integration (McNeil et al., 2012). Finally, more social justice-oriented programs with strong progressive missions may have a bias toward more oppressive aspects of religion. It is not surprising that resources on how to specifically navigate the ethical challenges of supporting spiritually and religiously healing practices while challenging hurtful practices remain lacking.

Influence of Clinician Values and Beliefs

A research study randomly surveyed AAMFT clinical members and found that 96% believed in a relationship between spiritual and mental health, while only 62% of participants believed spirituality should be considered in clinical practice (Carlson, Kirkpatrick, Hecker, & Killmer, 2002). This gap between understood impact on mental health and willingness to integrate spirituality and religion in clinical work is concerning. We know that clinicians' spiritual and religious beliefs powerfully influence attitudes and behaviors in therapy, the therapeutic relationship, and treatment outcomes (Cummings, Ivan, Carson, Stanley, Pargament, 2014).

We find that religious mental health clinicians tend to have more favorable attitudes toward integrating religion and spirituality into therapy, have more confidence in their ability to do so, and if affiliated with a specific group, are more likely to disclose personal beliefs to clients (Cummings et al., 2014). Clinicians high in religion are more likely to pray both overtly or covertly for their clients (Gubi, 2004) and are especially attentive to religion and spirituality in therapy, for example, using them in treatment goals (Cummings et al., 2014). Those high in religion also tend to hold conservative social values, do not support sexual minorities, and tend to be more aggressive toward and have difficulty connecting with clients violating traditional values (Williamson et al., 2010). They are more likely to diagnose sex addictions; view HIV-positive unprotected sex as more dangerous; disagree more with clients coming out as LGB; discourage premarital sex, abortions, and same-sex sexual behavior; and pathologize high levels of sexual behavior (Cummings et al., 2014). They may also be more reluctant to encourage clients to adopt distress-relieving behaviors or beliefs in conflict with their own or their client's beliefs (Cummings et al., 2014), for example, not teaching masturbation techniques when recommended in certain sex therapy interventions. Finally, highly religious clinicians prefer clients who share their values, though client-clinician religious similarity is not consistently related to therapeutic relationship or treatment outcome (Cummings et al., 2014).

Mental health clinicians low in religion seem to be guided primarily by clinical pragmatism and humanistic idealism and may overlook a client's relationship with the sacred or divine (Cummings et al., 2014). Nonreligious or low-in-religion clinicians feel more barriers to addressing spirituality (Cornish, Wade & Post, 2012) and are less likely to use spiritual and religious interventions (Shafranske & Malony, 1990). Clinicians low in religion, specializing with LGBTQ populations, are more likely to disagree with an adult client's goal of changing same-sex behavior or orientation (Cummings et al., 2014). Finally, clinicians low in religion may imply a client's religious beliefs and values are lower priorities than their subjective well-being, may avoid the topic of religion and spirituality, and are more likely to view religiousness as neurotic (Cummings et al., 2014).

A Post-oppositional Approach to Contextual Challenges

Given our polarizing societal discourses, challenges in clinical training, and some of the alarming practices of clinicians both high and low in religion, we need an ethical framework to guide our spiritual and religious interventions. We must understand the ethical implications of how we integrate religion and spirituality into clinical practice and possible societal inequities of clients' specific beliefs and practices. Toward this end, clinicians need a strong understanding of their own social location and need to process personal experiences and biases related to spirituality and religion. Research clearly shows clinicians are not neutral and need an ethical framework for how to use their therapeutic power. Evidence suggests that increasing helpful religious factors (i.e., religious hope and religious support) may be the solution to decreasing negative religious factors (i.e., negative beliefs, etc.) (Abu-Raiya, Pargament, & Krause, 2016). Drawing on social justice-, postmodern-, and critical-informed models (D'Arrigo-Patrick, Hoff, Knudson-Martin, & Tuttle, 2016), I created the *justice-informed framework for spiritual and religious resilience* that counters spiritually harmful beliefs and practices by collaborating with spiritually healing beliefs and practices. We can navigate the ethical tensions around who determines which beliefs are harmful or healing through a post-oppositional, co-created approach rooted in curiosity, which holds space for us to be partially right and wrong, and helps us stay in relationship (Keating, 2012).

Justice-Informed Framework for Spiritual and Religious Resilience (Fig. 1.1)

The *justice-informed framework for spiritual and religious resilience* invites clinicians to first assess client spiritual and religious coping, religious beliefs, community engagement, and societal context along a spectrum from potentially harmful to healing influences. As assessment unfolds, clinicians can begin to use their therapeutic power to open up new conversations and possibilities that challenge potentially hurtful practices and support healing practices.

Spiritual and Religious Assessment

Who we are as clinicians matters as we begin to assess our clients. Our own understandings and experiences of spirituality and religion influence us as do dominant discourses that privilege certain beliefs over other less acceptable beliefs. For example, beliefs such as those who seek God will find God, and morality now has eternal implications that are more permissible than beliefs in reincarnation, psychic communication, and shamanistic travels in other spiritual realms (Trimble, 2018). Ethical

Spiritual/Religious Assessment
Spiritual/religious coping
Spiritual/religious beliefs
Community engagement
Societal context

Harmful ←--→ Healing
Rigid, Shaming, Absent, Despairing *Hopeful, Loving, Relational, Empowering*

Therapeutic Activism
Counter ←--→ Collaborate
Challenge hurtful practices *Support healing practices*

Fig. 1.1 Justice-informed framework for spiritual/religious resilience, Esmiol Wilson

Table 1.1 Spiritual and religious assessment questions, Esmiol Wilson

Spiritual and religious assessment questions
Spiritual/religious coping
What is the role of your faith during difficult times?
How do you experience the divine or sacred during hard times?
Describe any spiritual/religious behaviors you might do when anxious or sad (e.g. pray, go to a religious service, read a holy text).
How do these spiritual/religious behaviors impact you and your relationships?
Spiritual/religious beliefs
What are some important spiritual/religious beliefs you hold?
How do your beliefs impact your relationships?
How do you image the divine or sacred sees you and feels about you?
Describe any beliefs you hold that feel difficult or conflicting.
Community engagement
Describe your connections or relationships within your faith community.
In what ways has your faith community impacted how you think about yourself?
How does your faith community support or hinder your beliefs and practices?
When might someone feel excluded in your religious community?
Societal context
How does the dominant culture support or marginalize your spiritual/religious beliefs?
What is the history of your religion regarding oppressing the beliefs of others?
How do your spiritual/religious beliefs potentially oppress or support others?
How does the intersection of your own social location (gender, sex, race, ethnicity, socioeconomic status, etc.) impact how you practice your beliefs?

assessments of both permissible and impermissible beliefs challenge us as practitioners to connect across difference and enter these spiritual spaces with humility and curiosity. I offer the following assessment questions as possible guides for collaboratively exploring the impact of client spirituality and religion on coping strategies, beliefs, spiritual/religious community, and the larger societal context (Table 1.1).

Therapeutic Activism: Counter and Collaborate

How do we hold a post-oppositional approach that makes room for multiple discourses and supports connection across difference while simultaneously challenging potentially harmful beliefs and practices? I think about those moments in my own clinical practice where collaboration and support make way for clients to courageously challenge their own rigid or long-held beliefs that are no longer working for them. I envision this sort of therapeutic activism as an invitation for clients to lean into their more empowering practices and listen closely to the more hopeful aspects of their own faith. I offer the following reflection questions and journaling prompts as possible invitations into expanded and more fulfilling ways of living out one's spirituality and religion (Table 1.2).

Table 1.2 Therapeutic activism: countering and collaborating questions, Esmiol Wilson

Therapeutic activism: countering and collaborating questions
Spiritual/religious coping
How can you resist spiritual/religious practices that do not support your well-being?
If you could imagine the divine or sacred inviting you into a place of rest, what would you need to let go of and what would you need to accept to say yes to this invitation?
What spiritual/religious practices might deepen your sense of self-worth and self-acceptance?
What specific spiritual/religious practices could lead you to increased integrity, generosity, and love?
Spiritual/religious beliefs
How can your beliefs heal feelings of guilt and shame and strengthen your sense of value and worth?
What would it look like for your spiritual/religious beliefs to support more honest and connected relationships with yourself, others, and the divine?
How can you defuse spiritual/religious beliefs that lead to division or fear, by expanding beliefs that offer connection and hope?
What spiritual/religious beliefs empower you toward a deeper sense of purpose?
Religious community
Describe what you would need to experience a sense of belonging within your religious community?
What would you need to feel valued and important within your religious community?
How could you connect with your religious community across difference, holding space for multiple perspectives?
Think of someone who might feel excluded in your religious community. What would it take to help this person feel more included? How would your answer differ if you were the one feeling included or excluded?
Societal context
How might you counter oppressive messages within the larger community that target your religious beliefs?
What difference would a deeper understanding of the history of your religion have in informing how you practice your beliefs?
If you could join or start more liberating movements within your own spiritual/religious community, what would they be?
How could you use your own intersection of social location (gender, sex, race, ethnicity, socioeconomic status, etc.) to support those potentially oppressed by your spirituality/religion?

Case Illustration: "I'm Afraid to Die"

Cindy and Rick, MFT interns in their first practicum at our on-site clinic, met with me weekly for supervision. Clinicians and client identities have been modified to protect confidentiality. Cindy, a 36-year-old Cambodian cisgender female student and single mother, was identified as culturally Buddhist. Rick, a 24-year-old white single cisgender male student, was raised in a new-age spiritual community and currently identified as atheist. I was a newly married white cisgender female assistant professor in my early 30s and had painfully disaffiliated from fundamental Evangelicalism but had not yet found a sense of community in progressive

Christianity. Their client, Alyssa, was a 42-year-old cisgender female wife and mother of five who was very active in her Latter-day Saints church. She had been diagnosed with terminal stage four breast cancer and came to therapy stating "I'm afraid to die and leave my children."

Critical Reflection of Self, Social Location, and Societal Context

Before encouraging Cindy and Rick to assess Alyssa's spiritual and religious coping, beliefs, and church community, I facilitated and modeled a critical self-reflection intended to keep diversity and oppression central in our discussion. Zimmerman, Castronova, and ChenFeng (2016) offer four primary areas to explore: Who are we? Who are the clients? How are we managing awareness of privilege, power, and bias? And how are we facilitating advocacy and change? As we explored these areas, two significant themes emerged around discomfort in attending to religion and distrust of religion as a helpful resource. Cindy spoke directly about her discomfort, "I'm not Christian like Dr. Wilson and Alyssa and really don't understand the Bible," yet she discounted her wisdom as a mother who could share more directly than Rick or I in Alyssa's experience as a mom. I voiced my own discomfort, sharing that currently being identified as a Christian felt incongruent as I was struggling with reevaluating my own faith, yet was conscious of not discounting my privilege as supervisor and as a graduate from a Christian seminary.

Rick spoke directly about his distrust of religion, sharing his experience of his mother who "always chose her spiritual group and their meditation rituals over attending any of my high school track meets." He struggled to see the positive relational aspects of religion but was open to leading any religious interventions, allowing Cindy to more comfortably suggest, "I could take a more supporting role." I wondered aloud about privileging Rick's white, male voice over Cindy's Cambodian, female voice and any possible impact on Alyssa of instead Rick supporting Cindy in leading the interventions. We also discussed Alyssa's seeming hesitancy in initiating any discussions about religion in therapy after learning neither of her clinicians were LDS, even though she marked her religion as "extremely important" to her and her treatment. We wondered about the clinician-client power imbalance and how Cindy and Rick might more directly create space for Alyssa to share the importance of her faith. I didn't process in supervision but consulted with a colleague about potential negative influences of my current faith struggles and my seminary experience which had trained me to identify the LDS faith or Mormonism as a cult. Only by identifying and returning to these supervisor-clinician-client intersecting social locations, embedded in our unique social contexts, were we able to manage our privilege, power, and bias and move toward assessment and treatment.

Assessment: Coping, Beliefs, Community, and Context

Cindy and Rick decided to divide their spiritual and religious assessment questions. After a session in which they invited Alyssa to talk about her religious life, they assessed that she experienced love and support from her religious community. Alyssa's sense of religious belonging seemed strengthened by her experience of feeling ostracized or "othered" as a Mormon, growing up in a more liberal area away from a robust LDS community. Cindy and Rick assessed that she seemed to be coping with her terminal diagnosis by reading her bible more and worrying over certain scripture passages about the "final judgment" and "salvation as conditional on obedience." Cindy and Rick also explored the meaning Alyssa was making about her diagnosis and her religious beliefs about death including her fear of death. Alyssa shared, "I'm not afraid of my own death. I'm afraid of dying because I don't want to leave my kids. I don't know what I'd do if even one of them stopped obeying God's commandments. I'd never see them again."

Therapeutic Activism: Countering and Collaborating

I supported Cindy and Rick in collaboratively exploring with Alyssa "what aspects of her current religious coping behaviors were or were not supporting a sense of peace and well-being." Alyssa identified that praying and singing hymns about God's faithfulness brought her more peace, but reading scripture about salvation from sin seemed to increase her anxiety about leaving her kids when she died. In supervision, we wondered about Alyssa seeming to have a hard time accessing grief about her terminal diagnosis and how her religious coping might be distancing her from sadness. As Cindy and Rick shared this possibility with curiosity during the fifth session, Alyssa started to cry and later shared, "I think that was the first time I really let myself feel sad."

Alyssa found journaling to be particularly helpful, especially on the question: "How can you defuse spiritual/religious beliefs that lead to division or fear, by expanding beliefs that offer connection and hope?" From supervision to therapy, conversations focused on holding a post-oppositional stance that made room for Alyssa to draw on multiple beliefs. As she leaned into her deep beliefs about God's love and faithfulness, she began holding more hope for her children and more trust in God's power to support her husband and their religious community in bringing up her children without her. As Alyssa became more grounded in supportive religious coping and beliefs, she invited her husband and then finally her children for a few family therapy sessions to process their grief and talk about ways to hold onto love. After a total of 18 sessions, Alyssa became too weak to attend therapy. Six months later, Alyssa's husband came back for one session to express how much Cindy and Rick had meant to his wife. He shared that Alyssa had died peacefully surrounded by her five children. In supervision, Cindy and Rick reflected on how deeply they had been touched by knowing Alyssa. Cindy realized she had found not only more confidence but a deep passion for integrating spirituality and religion into therapy, and Rick's experience had revealed the power of a loving, hopeful faith in supporting family resilience.

Application of Framework

My hope is that this *justice-informed framework* supports clinicians in critically thinking about how we are utilizing our therapeutic power in supporting and countering our clients' spirituality and religion. The following chapters utilize and apply this framework to various clinical populations and presenting issues. Through the following clinical and personal examples, this book illustrates the importance of directing addressing and integrating spirituality and religion into treatment. I hope you will find the inspiration and guidance in the following pages to use your voice to expand such sacred conversations in the therapy room.

References

Abu-Raiya, H., Pargament, K. I., & Krause, N. (2016). Religion as problem, religion as solution: religious buffers of the links between religious/spiritual struggles and well-being/mental health. *Quality of Life Research: An International Journal of Quality of Life Aspects of Treatment, Care and Rehabilitation, 25*(5), 1265–1274.

Baker, P., & Cruickshank, J. (2010). I am happy in my faith: The influence of religious affiliation, saliency, and practice on depressive symptoms and treatment preference. *Mental Health, Religion & Culture, 12*, 339–357.

Bhalla, N. (2018). Rare win for gay rights as Kenya court rules forced anal tests illegal. *Thomson Reuters Foundation*. Retrieved from http://news.trust.org

Carlson, T., McGeorge, C., & Toomey, R. (2014). Establishing the validity of the spirituality in clinical training scale: Measuring the level of integration of spirituality and religion in family therapy training. *Contemporary Family Therapy: An International Journal, 36*(2), 310–325.

Carlson, T. D., Kirkpatrick, D., Hecker, L., & Killmer, M. (2002). Religion, spirituality, and marriage and family therapy: A study of family therapists' beliefs about the appropriateness of addressing religious and spiritual issues in therapy. *American Journal of Family Therapy, 30*(2), 157–171.

Cattich, J., & Knudson-Martin, C. (2009). Spirituality and relationship: A holistic analysis of how couples cope with diabetes. *Journal of Marital and Family Therapy, 35*(1), 111–124.

Cornish, M. A., Wade, N. G., & Post, B. C. (2012). Attending to religion and spirituality in group counseling: Counselors' perceptions and practices. *Group Dynamics: Theory, Research and Practice, 16*, 122–137.

Coyle, S. M. (2017). Integrating spirituality in marriage and family therapy training. *Australian and New Zealand Journal of Family Therapy, 38*(1), 142–155.

Cummings, J. P., Ivan, M. C., Stanley, M. A., & Pargament, K. I. (2014). A systemic review of relations between psychotherapist religiousness/spirituality and therapy-related variables. *Spirituality in Clinical Practice, 1*(2), 116–132.

D'Arrigo-Patrick, J., Hoff, C., Knudson-Martin, C., & Tuttle, A. (2016). Navigating critical theory and postmodernism: Social justice and therapist power in family therapy. *Family Process, 56*(3), 574–588.

Esmiol Wilson, E., Knudson-Martin, C., & Wilson, C. (2014). Gendered power, spirituality, and relational processes: Experiences of Christian physician couples. *Journal of Couple and Relationship Therapy, 13*(4), 312–338.

George, L. K., Larsons, D. B., Koeing, H. G., & McCullough, M. E. (2000). Spirituality and health: What we know, what we need to know. *Journal of Social and Clinical Psychology, 19*(1), 102–116.

Giblin, P. R. (2004). Marital health and spirituality. *Journal of Pastoral Counseling, 39*, 43–67.

Gubi, P. M. (2004). Surveying the extent of, and attitudes towards, the use of prayer as a spiritual intervention among British mainstream counsellors. *British Journal of Guidance & Counselling, 32*, 461–476.

Hall, T. W., & Fujikawa, A. M. (2013). God image and the sacred. In K. I. Pargament, J. J. Exline, J. W. Jones, K. I. Pargament, J. J. Exline, & J. W. Jones (Eds.), *APA handbook of psychology, religion, and spirituality (Vol 1): Context, theory, and research* (pp. 277–292). Washington, DC: American Psychological Association.

Hill, P. C., & Hood, R. W. (1999). Affect, religion and unconscious process. *Journal of Personality, 67*(6), 1015–1046.

Hughes, P. C., & Dickson, F. C. (2005). Communication, marital satisfaction, and religious orientation in interfaith marriages. *Journal of Family Communication, 5*(1), 25–41.

Keating, A. (2012). *Transformation now! Toward a post-oppositional politics of change*. Chicago: University of Illinois Press.

Kirkpatrick, L. A., & Hood, R. W. (1990). Intrinsic-extrinsic religious orientation: The boon or bane of contemporary psychology of religion? *Journal for the Scientific Study of Religion, 29*(4), 422–463.

Marterella, M. K., & Brock, L. J. (2008). Religion and spirituality as a resource in marital and family therapy. *Journal of Family Psychotherapy, 19*(4), 330–344.

McGeorge, C., Carlson, T., & Toomey, R. (2014). The intersection of spirituality, religion, sexual orientation, and gender identity in family therapy training: An exploration of students' beliefs and practices. *Contemporary Family Therapy: An International Journal, 36*(4), 497–506.

McNeil, S., Pavkov, T., Hecker, L., & Killmer, J. (2012). Marriage and family therapy graduate students' satisfaction with training regarding religion and spirituality. *Contemporary Family Therapy: An International Journal, 34*(4), 468–480.

Pargament, K. I. (2007). *Spiritually integrated psychotherapy: Understanding and addressing the sacred*. New York: Guilford Press.

Shafranske, E. P., & Malony, H. N. (1990). Clinical psychologists' religious and spiritual orientations and their practice of psychotherapy. *Psychotherapy: Theory, Research, Practice, Training, 27*, 72.

Slater, W., Hall, T. W., & Edwards, K. J. (2003). Measuring religion and spirituality: Where are we and where are we going? In T. W. Hall & M. R. McMinn (Eds.), *Spiritual formation, counseling, and psychotherapy* (pp. 235–260). Hauppauge, NY: Nova Science Publishers.

Trimble, D. (2018). From the margins to the center: Generative possibilities in multicultural dialogue on spirituality. In D. Trimble (Ed.), *Engaging with spirituality in family therapy: Meeting in sacred space* (pp. 1–13). AFTA Springer Brief.

Walsh, F. (2009). Religion and spirituality in couple and family relations. In J. H. Bray & M. Stanton (Eds.), *The Wiley-Blackwell handbook of family psychology* (pp. 600–612). Hoboken, NJ: Wiley-Blackwell.

Weber, S. R., & Pargament, K. I. (2014). The role of religion and spirituality in mental health. *Current Opinion in Psychiatry, 27*(5), 358–363.

Weber, S. R., Pargament, K. I., Kunik, M. E., Lomax, J. W., & Stanley, M. A. (2012). Psychological distress among religious nonbelievers: A systematic review. *Journal of Religion and Health, 51*(1), 72–86.

Weiler, L. M., Lyness, K. P., Haddock, S. A., & Zimmerman, T. S. (2015). Contextual issues in couple and family therapy: Gender, sexual orientation, culture, and spirituality. In J. L. Wetchler, L. L. Hecker, J. L. Wetchler, & L. L. Hecker (Eds.), *An introduction to marriage and family therapy* (pp. 65–116). New York: Routledge/Taylor & Francis Group.
Williamson, W., Hood, R., Ahmad, A., Sadiq, M., & Hill, P. C. (2010). The intratextual fundamentalism scale: Cross-cultural application, validity evidence, and relationship with religious orientation and the big 5 factor markers. *Mental Health, Religion & Culture, 13*, 721–747.
Zimmerman, T., Castronova, M., & ChenFeng, J. (2016). Diversity and social justice in supervision. In K. Jordan & K. Jordan (Eds.), *Couple, marriage, and family therapy supervision* (pp. 121–148). New York: Springer Publishing.

Chapter 2
Integration of Self and Family: Asian American Christians in the Midst of White Evangelicalism and Being the Model Minority

Jessica L. ChenFeng

I have a small private practice in South Pasadena, a small city on the west end of the San Gabriel Valley (SGV), which is located in Los Angeles County, California. The San Gabriel Valley is home to well over half a million Asian Americans; this is more Asian Americans than in 42 states as well as in the cities of Los Angeles, San Francisco, and Chicago. From 2000 to 2010, the Asian American population grew 22%, which is three times as fast as any other racial group in the San Gabriel Valley (Asian Americans Advancing Justice, 2018). In this context, I have established my practice, which serves mostly second-generation Asian Americans, particularly women and women who identify with having an evangelical Christian heritage.

The religious demographics of the Asian American population are not common knowledge. Forty-two percent of all Asian Americans in the United States identify as Christian (including Protestant, Catholic, and other Christians) and are more committed than all US Christians (Pew Research Center, 2012). For example, 61% say they attend religious services at least once a week (vs. 45% of all US Christians) and are more likely to say that living a very religious life is one of their most important goals (37% vs. 24%). Those who identify as evangelical Protestants have the highest self-reported service attendance rates with 76% going to service at least once a week.

Many of my clients grew up in an Asian American evangelical context, and in the SGV there are many Asian American Christian churches. At the time they seek therapy, clients may be on a different leg of their spiritual journey – some are still regularly attending and serving in church, others no longer attend, and some are trying to integrate the religious context of their upbringing with changing social realities. The intention of this chapter is to introduce you to these clients, their context, and the clinical work we do together, weaving conversations of cultural heritage, spirituality, gender, and race.

J. L. ChenFeng (✉)
University Medical Center, Loma Linda University, Loma Linda, CA, USA
e-mail: Jchenfeng@llu.edu

E. Esmiol Wilson, L. Nice (eds.), *Socially Just Religious and Spiritual Interventions*, AFTA SpringerBriefs in Family Therapy, https://doi.org/10.1007/978-3-030-01986-0_2

Social Location and Reasons for Seeking Therapy

I identify as an Asian American Christian woman that was born and raised and still resides in the San Gabriel Valley. My clients are women in their late 20s to mid-30s, come from middle-class families, are in graduate school or at the start of their careers, are single and dating as well as married, and identify as heterosexual. While I have facilitated group therapy for Asian American Queer Christians, this chapter focuses on the experience of Asian American Christian heterosexual cisgender women of East and Southeast Asian heritages.

There are a few common presenting concerns with which these women come to therapy. One area of interest is their desire to work on their sense of self; whether related to family of origin dynamics or through dating and relationship challenges, they experience themselves as having a difficult time with establishing boundaries and speaking up. The other is a general presentation of depression and anxiety, usually related to family dynamics, dating, and their work context.

Clinical Foundation

During the 1st year of my training, my clinical supervisor trained us to apply Bowen family systems theory to our cases. I have always appreciated the concepts of differentiation and family genogram work as these inform much of how I understand individuals and their family context. Bowen family systems theory's strength is in assessing the levels of anxiety and reactivity in families (Titelman, 1998). It believes that the family system plays out a multigenerational transmission process where differentiation levels of family members can increase or decrease from generation to generation. Differentiation is the ability to identify one's own thoughts and feelings separately from that of the family. A higher level of differentiation tends to be related to less relational distress, as differentiation increases, anxiety decreases, and the presenting problems can begin to modify or disappear (Titelman). Clinical intervention focuses on encouraging each person to recognize his or her own sensitivity to others and the automatic feeling states and behaviors that are associated with these sensitivities (Papero, 1990).

The other theory that informs my practice is Socio-emotional Relationship Therapy (SERT). It is a model of therapy that provides understanding about emotions being tied to sociocultural contexts (Knudson-Martin & Huenergardt, 2010). Though many of its guiding principles are initially intended to be applied in couples' therapy, they are also relevant for working with larger contextual issues across multiple relationship dynamics. Practitioners of this therapy believe that cultural and societal discourses shape how and what emotions are expressed, and these cultural messages are connected to the intersecting power dynamics related to one's social location (Knudson-Martin & Huenergardt, 2015).

Through an internal grant at the California State University, Northridge, I studied my own clinical processes and came up with the concept of *contextual differentiation* (ChenFeng, 2018), which seems to highlight the work I do with my clients. If individual differentiation is the ability to identify one's own thoughts and feelings separately from that of the family, then contextual differentiation is identifying one's own thoughts and feelings as they are influenced by, related to, or different from one's context. The challenge is that most clients do not know the various contexts in which they are embedded. In this next section, I will discuss the multiple sociocultural contexts relevant to clinical work with this population.

Exploring Sociocultural Contexts

In my clinical work, I navigate conversations with clients across four main sociocultural contexts: immigration history and trauma, the larger American context, the evangelical context, and their family context. These four contexts are interconnected. The disconnect clients live with, in not knowing about or understanding these contexts, influences of their experiences of relational ruptures, depression, and anxiety.

Immigration History and Trauma

These second-generation Asian American women have parents who immigrated from their countries of origin, each family with its own story of loss and resilience. For some first-generation parents, sharing their immigration stories is possible because they have somehow arrived at their own coherent narratives and can convey these to their children. For many first-generation parents, however, weaving a coherent narrative is out of reach due to such significant trauma and loss in the family's journey to the United States. The second generation is not able to fully recognize and process their family's loss and grief, a process hampered by sociocultural and historical reasons (Park-Hearn, 2017). Clients have expressed to me these sentiments of feeling their parents' grief, loss, or anxiety but never having access to hearing their parents' experiences. This creates a generational disconnect (ChenFeng, Knudson-Martin, & Nelson, 2015) that seems impossible to bridge.

This generational disconnect around family history and trauma is only one of many areas of disconnect. The collective experience of feeling disconnected from parents and one's family and cultural narrative contributes to feelings of loss, division, and depression. One of the activities I encourage is for clients to find a way to connect to either their personal immigration history or the larger collective stories of Asian American immigration experiences. Sometimes it is possible for clients to ask their parents, an aunt, uncle, or extended family member about why and how the family came to the United States. Clients typically come back to session energized, amazed, and feeling more deeply connected to their family and heritage. They can make better sense of their parents' personalities and inclinations (i.e., being strict or anxiety-prone) through empathizing about family grief, experiences of discrimination, their parents' resilience, and perseverance.

If it is not possible to connect directly with family, I might suggest books, movies, articles, or websites that speak to the stories of Asian American immigrants (www.asian-nation.org offers historical and demographic information; Erika Lee's *The Making of Asian America: A History* is a great resource (Lee, 2015)). When clients recognize their own family experiences through other narratives, there is a sense of relief, belonging, and connectedness to the Asian American experience. This is powerful in relieving the feelings of isolation and aloneness that lead to depression. Contextual differentiation is raised through being able to identify one's own position in relation to their family, their family's history, a history of being colonized or perpetrated against, and the larger Asian American story.

The Larger American Context

There are many racialized messages that Asian Americans live within the larger American context. Two such stereotypes are those of being the *model minority* (Peterson, 1996) and the *forever foreigner* (Tuan, 1998).

> As Asian American scholars point out, the model minority construct is only a surface manifestation of the underlying struggles and anxieties in America's racialized society. The model minority construct functions as a mechanism – checks and balances – to control or maneuver the racialized playing field. The ideological transaction of garnering the model minority prize creates a relationship between Asian Americans and dominant white society whereby in exchange for coming first among non-white ethnic groups Asian Americans continue the foreigner status; quietly remain respectful and obedient to the authorities; and enable the racialized instrumentalism of Asian Americans. (Yu, 2016, p. 5–6)

Many Asian Americans feel the pressure to live up to the model minority construct – being exemplary students and employees who "quietly remain respectful and obedient" (Yu, 2016). This is magnified for Asian American women who also wrestle with expectations to be submissive and modest. Sometimes my clients will express frustration and stress around how to speak up in their classrooms or workplaces. The tension is this: "I was raised to be respectful of authority which often translates to staying silent in the midst of disagreement but attempting to appear agreeable. I also don't want to give off a bad reputation for Asian Americans by being loud and disagreeing with my boss." Both family and intracultural expectations as well as pressure to maintain a particular Asian American identity to the larger dominant culture paralyze clients to speak up and express their opinions.

Being the *forever foreigner* means that regardless of generational status or cultural practice, Asian Americans are perceived to be foreigners because of their phenotypical presentation. Even someone identified as a fourth-generation Chinese American, speaking only English and raised in an "Americanized" family, will still be asked "Where are you from?" This exacerbates feelings of being on the outside, of not belonging; no matter how hard one tries to be accepted as "American," they remain on the margins of society.

Most of my clients are generally aware of these stereotypes but do not know how they influence their day-to-day lived experience as Asian Americans. Day after day, year after year of being in multiple contexts that reinforce such messages can erode one's sense of self. Without understanding the historical, sociopolitical forces behind these racialized stereotypes, clients can remain in a state of disempowerment.

When clients share about such experiences, I spend a lot of time validating the complex emotions and thoughts that come with them. It is critical for me to be familiar with literature on how racism and discrimination impacts health and identity. It is helpful to validate clients' experiences through referencing the research: "Of course you are tired and your body hurts. We know from studies on the experiences of racism that it takes a toll on people's physical health." Clients may not be familiar with the specific terms *model minority* or *forever foreigner* (or any other racialization of Asian Americans) so as I hear them say something reflective of these stereotypes and I normalize their experiences through sharing about these constructs. Clients are typically surprised that there are terms for their experiences and feel seen and heard. They also report feeling like they are not alone because other Asian Americans have similar experiences and can resonate.

As clients start to understand the historical context of racism against Asian Americans, they are better able to understand their own emotional responses in light of others' discriminatory remarks or gestures. A female client may reflect on raised contextual differentiation by saying something like, "I get so pissed that my white male colleague keeps telling me I'm cute. Knowing the context of the objectification of Asian women helps me understand why this always happens to me and I feel like I can tell him I don't like it, and explain why instead of shrink away, which felt so terrible."

The Evangelical Context

Because my clients come from mostly Asian American evangelical contexts, this also means they were very much influenced by white heteropatriarchy. Many second-generation Asian American Christians are put off by their parents placing Asian culture above the church, so they:

> promote a culture-free and color-blind church, a position on race shared with white evangelicalism... What emerges is the self-reinforcement of the Christian model minority: the maintenance of white privilege, affirmation of middle-class standing, preservation of ethnic hierarchy in American evangelicalism, and compliance in the racialized formation of Asian Americans. (Yu, 2016, pg. 3–4)

Growing up in the Asian American evangelical church makes it more likely for young Asian Americans to think that they should not think about their racial identity and how it intersects with their spirituality. What is more overt is the discussion of gender, often a mix of theology and patriarchy shaping family life and individual identity. My clients grew up in homes where father was the head of household, both for cultural and religious reasons. They saw their mothers and women in the church submit to men, sometimes to harmful extremes. Christian religious discourses to "persevere" or that "suffering makes one more like Jesus" perpetuate women's status as remaining one down.

In session, we might use the genogram to map what patriarchy looks like in their current relationships with men (i.e., the critical genogram, which explores how systems of oppression shape experience; Garcia, Kosutic, & Barnett, 2008). Understanding that their relational patterns are connected to the social context in which they grew up frees them from feeling stuck around thoughts such as "I don't know why I always get into these types of relationships" or "How come I can't speak up or express my preferences to the people I date?"

A helpful activity is asking if the client knows of a couple or another Asian American Christian woman who is in a more mutual egalitarian relationship. I encourage the client to spend time with the couple or the friend and be curious about the dynamics of their relationship. This allows the client to envision how an Asian American Christian woman can be different from what she saw modeled growing up and to witness different theological understandings of gender relationships. It gives her courage to imagine herself in a relational dynamic where she can be attuned to her own needs and expect her partner to also do so.

Talking about race and patriarchy as they relate to the evangelical church facilitates the raising of contextual differentiation and gives the client permission to consider these issues as sociocultural influences which can be more fluid, as opposed to fixed theological beliefs (Esmiol Wilson, 2018).

The Family Context

There is an Asian American values scale (Kim, Li, & Ng, 2005) that provides a general idea of the values important to Asian Americans. The scale highlights six Asian cultural value dimensions: collectivism, conformity to norms, emotional self-control, family recognition through achievement, filial piety, and humility (Kim, Yang, Atkinson, Wolfe, & Hong, 2001).

Collectivism is the emphasis on considering the group's needs before one's own needs; it means seeing one's own achievement as equivalent to the family's achievement. Many second-generation individuals consider their family's concerns and well-being as they make life decisions. *Conformity to norms* means conforming to social expectations such as those that are significant to the family and fulfilling expected gender roles; it places significance on refraining from bringing disgrace to the family. *Emotional self-control* is valued because it means having the capacity to control emotions; one is expected to have the internal resources to resolve emotional issues and have unspoken understanding about emotional needs. *Family recognition through achievement* is the importance of avoiding shaming the family by being successful in academic and occupational endeavors. *Filial piety* refers to a deep respect of parents and elders as having greater wisdom than those younger as well as taking care of parents' needs when they are older. It means refraining from speaking back to parents or expressing disagreement. *Humility* is the emphasis on holding on to modesty and refraining from being boastful. It is more acceptable to modestly put oneself down and not express competence. This is particularly expected of women.

These core six values undergird the lives of Asian American families. Oftentimes these values are not spoken of or overtly taught. *When I tell clients about these values, they feel validation that research has acknowledged and defined such personal familial values.*

One common mistake clinicians might make is to think that these values are lived out in Asian American families as though they are fixed values without influence from the sociocultural context around them. Present-day family life is impacted by the family immigration story and history, the larger American context, and the white heteropatriarchy of the evangelical church. I encourage clients to talk to their siblings or other Asian American friends about how they experience these values in family life. We also explore why a family or the first-generation parents might particularly esteem one or two of these values, leading to the second-generation adult child feeling pressure and stress.

As the client begins to formulate a story around how these contexts – immigration history, the larger American context, and the white evangelical world – influence their family's experiences and relationships, there is an increased sense of connection to parents and their Asian American identity.

Case Study

Sarah is a 31-year-old second-generation Korean American woman who was referred to me by a local colleague. She is in the 2nd year of a master's in marriage and family therapy program and thought it was a good time to get some therapy because she says "I have issues with dating and don't know if I'm in the right field." Lately she has been feeling down and also reports having a difficult time with a supervisor at her internship site.

Sarah's parents immigrated from South Korea in the mid-1980s and joined Sarah's uncle's family in Orange County, California. The city in which they live has sizeable Asian American and Korean American populations. She has always known that her father's family was from North Korea and that she still had relatives that were left there but she never heard stories about what happened. While her mother's family seems to connect and talk often, her father does not talk much about family.

Sarah's parents opened a Korean restaurant shortly after she was born and have always been active at their local fairly large-sized Korean Christian church, which Sarah and her brother grew up attending. John is Sarah's older brother by 3 years and is finishing up his last year of law school.

As we began our work together, Sarah's work environment and relationship with her supervisor seemed to be most pressing. I explored the dynamics around her work environment: the racial backgrounds of and dynamics between her supervisors, colleagues, and clients. I learned that Sarah is the only Asian American intern at the site with mostly white supervisors and Latino clients. Her supervisor seemed to be getting frustrated with Sarah for not being more direct with the clients who needed to learn parenting skills. She felt stressed about how to be "more direct" to clients who were older than she was, especially because she did not have any children herself.

In our conversations, we unpacked her experience of living up to the model minority construct, talked about the important Asian American Christian values she grew up with and how it felt disrespectful to speak in the way her supervisor wanted. We also discussed the communication styles in her workplace and how she felt so different and stressed every time she wanted to speak up but did not know how to interject her voice. One of the powerful areas of exploration was examining her academic and training context – how much consideration for her ethnic and cultural identity was a part of her learning? We learned that her supervisor cared about social justice issues but perhaps was not aware of how to thoughtfully mentor an Asian American intern. Sarah could be outspoken in other contexts but felt conflicted about doing so with her supervisor. We role-played possible ways of communicating with her supervisor that felt more congruent with her identity and that would convey how she was experiencing supervision. Being able to identify her thoughts and feelings as they were related to her experiences with microaggressions and marginalization was grounding for her.

Sarah grew up sensing that her brother had some sort of privileged status in the extended family because their father was the firstborn son, and John was the first grandson. Even though her parents would never dare to say this, she could tell that their parents placed some sort of greater value on John by the things he got away with and that as the daughter she could never point out this difference in treatment. At church, she grew up witnessing male pastoral leadership, while the women ran the children's ministries and took care of food preparation. At home, her father was temperamental and would have intimidating anger outbursts when the house was messy or if he was stressed about finances. Her mother would tell the children to help clean the house before dad got home and made sure dinner was ready.

While we worked together, Sarah had just ended another dating relationship. She talked about being attracted to "manly" men, men who had strong personalities and knew what they wanted. She did not understand why she was always left feeling stepped on, minimized, and like she always had to cater to their needs. We spent time working on a genogram exploring her family's history, and she was able to connect with an aunt who shared more about her father's family story. We engaged around the cultural patriarchy, the trauma, and the disconnect, as well as the resilience, perseverance, and hope. We spent some time discussing patriarchy, the rules of "being a man" or "being a woman" in the Korean American Christian context. We briefly touched upon how many of the Korean American male pastors were reading from and teaching from texts written by white male evangelical pastors and how this might have influenced her upbringing in the church.

Sarah was able to connect with some friends who married "feminist" husbands and expressed surprise and delight at the possibility of having such a relationship. She started to better understand how her family and church context influenced her emotions and attractions around dating, which began to shift during our work together.

Toward the end of our therapeutic relationship, Sarah was able to put together the pieces of her family's story in context. She had increased empathy for her parents and the layers of loss they encountered growing up and in immigration. There were even a few occasions she had conversations with them about their upbringing in Korea and what it was like to move to another country. Her greatest insight was around seeing the mix of pressure from so many angles: the American context telling her to succeed and live up to the model minority family image, the Christian church context where her dad had social status to maintain as an elder, and the Korean context where it was important to remain faithful to Korean values as a way of holding on to their ethnic identity when so much else had been stripped away. Sarah's parents were not simply "rigid Asian parents" who had issues because they were not "acculturated enough." This narrative, too often believed by Asian Americans, further disconnects second-generation children from their parents and deepens the internalized racism. Sarah was not a bad daughter for feeling resentment or guilt because her parents did not value her career in the same way as that of her brother's. Reenvisioning their emotions, thoughts, and reactions to one another in light of their sociocultural context liberated Sarah from judging her parents, believing that her cultural ways of being were subpar, and trying to become more like "them" (ideal Christian woman as defined by white Evangelicalism and the ideal white therapist).

Clinical Implications

The following clinical recommendations are for therapists working specifically with Asian American Christian populations:

Learn About Contextualized Asian American Christian History and Identity

As with working with any population, it is critical for the therapist to have a *working knowledge base about Asian American history and identity as it relates to the larger American context.* There is of course no one way that identities of marginalization – be it race, ethnicity, gender, spirituality/religion, and class – impact individuals and families. Taking the time to read about and become acquainted with the complexities of this community is necessary. Particularly important are the influences of whiteness/American context, white Evangelicalism, and patriarchy.

Hold Space for Unique, Ever-Shifting Experiences

What often happens in "cultural competence" training is education about certain populations as though they have a particular set of cultural values, norms, and family structures, and then there are clinical interventions that correspond to these. Each individual and familial experience is unique to their context, ever-shifting and interacting with their societal context. While it is important to have the working knowledge base mentioned above, it is just as important to *hold this loosely and take in each clients' experience as it shifts, transforms, and is shaped by their experience.*

Hold Space for Both Loss and Resilience

Holding the tension between validating clients' loss/grief and their resilience is part of the way forward. Families of color with immigration histories have intergenerational tension and layers of grief that are often unseen and unacknowledged. Giving words to their experience and feelings is important while at the same time recognizing the amazing ways by which families have survived and fought to thrive.

Help Families Reenvision Their Experiences in Light of the Larger Sociocultural Context

Lastly, working with Asian American families who have a Christian heritage is not merely an issue of addressing their ethnic and religious identities. *The contextual differentiation* framework considers the multiple layered contexts of an individual or family's identity and raises critical consciousness around each context. As clients raise their contextual differentiation, they are freed to choose to live as integrated whole persons instead of disconnected on the margins.

References

Asian Americans Advancing Justice (2018). *A community of contrasts: Asian Americans, Native Hawaiians, and Pacific Islanders in the San Gabriel Valley.* Retrieved from https://advancingjustice-la.org/sites/default/files/A_Community_of_Contrasts_ SGV_2018.pdf

ChenFeng, J. (2018). *Relational wellness for second generation Asian American adult children.* Presentation at the California State University, Northridge, Northridge, CA.

ChenFeng, J., Knudson-Martin, C., & Nelson, T. (2015). Intergenerational tension, connectedness and separateness in the lived experience of first and second generation Chinese American Christians. *Contemporary Family Therapy: An International Journal, 37*(2), 153–164. https://doi.org/10.1007/s10591-015-9335-9

Esmiol Wilson, E. (2018). From assessment to activism: Utilizing a justice-informed framework to guide spiritual and religious clinical interventions. In E. Esmiol Wilson & L. A. Nice (Eds.), *Socially just religious and spiritual interventions: Ethical uses of therapeutic power, AFTA Springer Briefs*. Cham, Switzerland: Springer.

Garcia, M., Kosutic, I., & Barnett, F. (2008). The critical genogram: A tool for developing critical consciousness. *PsycEXTRA Dataset*. https://doi.org/10.1037/e506102012-140

Kim, B. S. K., Li, L., & Ng, G. F. (2005). The Asian American values scale – multidimensional: Development, reliability, and validity. *Cultural Diversity & Ethnic Minority Psychology, 11*(3), 187–201.

Kim, B. S. K., Yang, P. H., Atkinson, D. R., Wolfe, M. M., & Hong, S. (2001). Cultural value similarities and differences among Asian American ethnic groups. *Cultural Diversity and Ethnic Minority Psychology, 7*(4), 343–361.

Knudson-Martin, C., & Huenergardt, D. (2010). A socio-emotional approach to couple therapy: Linking social context and couple interaction. *Family Process, 49*(3), 369–384.

Knudson-Martin, C., & Huenergardt, D. (2015). Bridging emotion, societal discourse, and couple interaction in clinical practice. In C. Knudson-Martin, M. Wells, & S. Samman (Eds.), *Socio-emotional relationship therapy: Bridging emotional, societal context, and couple interaction* (pp. 1–13). New York: Springer.

Lee, E. (2015). *The making of Asian America: A history*. New York, NY: Simon & Schuster.

Papero, D. (1990). *Bowen family systems theory*. Boston, MA: Allyn and Bacon.

Park-Hearn, J. (2017). Prayers of lament: Making space for our disenfranchised grief. *ChristianityNext, 1*, 67–93.

Petersen, W. (1996, January 9). Success story, Japanese-American style. *The New York Times Magazine.*

Pew Research Center (2012). *Asian Americans: A mosaic of faiths.* Retrieved from http://www.pewforum.org/2012/07/19/asian-americans-a-mosaic-of-faiths-overview/

Titelman, P. (Ed.). (1998). *Clinical applications of Bowen family systems theory*. New York: The Haworth Press.

Tuan, M. (1998). *Forever foreigners or honorary whites?* Piscataway, NJ: Rutgers University Press.

Yu, K. K. (2016). Christian model minority: Racial and ethnic formation in Asian American evangelicalism. *Journal of Race, Ethnicity, and Religion, 7*(4), 1–24.

Chapter 3
Protecting Family Bonds: Examining Religious Disaffiliation Through a Spiritually Informed Family Systems Lens

April Knight, Elisabeth Esmiol Wilson, and Lindsey Nice

Introduction

Over the past 20 years, significantly more US citizens identify as nonreligious (Kosmin & Keysar, 2009; Smith, Marsden, Hout, & Kim, 2011; Vargas, 2012). Religious disaffiliation, defined as the process of leaving a formerly practiced religion, largely contributes to this increase. In one study, researchers found that 13% of religiously affiliated Americans seriously considered disaffiliating from religion during the years of 2003–2006 (Vargas). Additionally, almost all religious people experience some fluctuation in their religious beliefs and/or level of participation over the course of their lifetime (Fisher, 2016). Leaving a family religion is often a complex process that can significantly impact the individual disaffiliating as well as family members and family relationships. Experiences of grief, emotional distress, and PTSD symptoms can impact both the disaffiliating and still affiliated family members (Beder, 2004; Winell, 2007). Given the often difficult emotional and systemic impact of religious disaffiliation, clinicians need guidelines for working with families during these religious transitions.

This chapter draws on the somewhat limited body of research examining the process and impact of religious disaffiliation. Utilizing this literature and a study we co-conducted, we will describe why and how people disaffiliate as well as the systemic impact of disaffiliation. Based on our clinical work, we provide a case example to illustrate one family's experience of the individual and relational impacts of religious disaffiliation within their family system. Guided by interpersonal neurobiological,

A. Knight (✉)
Private Marriage and Family Therapy Practice, Tacoma, WA, USA

E. Esmiol Wilson · L. Nice
Marriage and Family Therapy Program, Pacific Lutheran University, Tacoma, WA, USA

E. Esmiol Wilson, L. Nice (eds.), *Socially Just Religious and Spiritual Interventions*, AFTA SpringerBriefs in Family Therapy, https://doi.org/10.1007/978-3-030-01986-0_3

feminist family therapy and socially just religious/spiritual care in therapy models (see Esmiol Wilson, 2018), we conclude with clinical implications for better guiding families through transitions of religious disaffiliation.

Social Location and Approach to Research

I (April) am a White, heterosexual, cisgender female and have experienced several reconfigurations of faith over the course of my life as I have adapted to new information, experiences, and environments. I actively participate in my faith community, The Church of Jesus Christ of Latter-day Saints (LDS), and am a practicing marriage and family therapist committed to advocating for social justice. These two paths are complimentary in many ways; yet there are times when beliefs or values diverge and standing in the tension is challenging. Two of my brothers disaffiliated from the LDS church, while two siblings remain. My former spouse disaffiliated in the 13th year of our marriage, which ultimately contributed to our divorce. We try to make room for differing religious perspectives as we co-parent our children. We (Elisabeth and Lindsey) are White, heterosexual, cisgender female faculty members who worked with April on her study when she was our student. I (Elisabeth) attend progressive reconciling ministries United Methodist Church, and I (Lindsey) am part of a Seventh-day Adventist congregation.

We conducted a qualitative research project utilizing grounded theory analytic procedures to examine religious disaffiliation through a family systems lens. Our sample of 12 participants consisted of 5 family systems, representing 5 different Christian denominations: Catholic, Latter-day Saint (Mormon), Methodist, Pentecostal, and Seventh-day Adventist. We used in-depth interviews to gather data on research questions addressing the individual's experience of the disaffiliation and the impact they saw on family relationships. The stories collected from these five families inform our clinical work and echo some of our own experiences of navigating these transitions.

Guiding Clinical Theories

Feminist Family Therapy

Feminist family therapy guides our work with families who are navigating the sometimes-turbulent relational shifts that occur during the religious disaffiliation process. While systems theory focuses on the interconnected and interdependent nature of human relationships, the feminist lens highlights inequities of power and privilege within systems and disperses responsibility accordingly. Feminist family therapy helps us recognize and challenge unhelpful inequities. In our research, participants often reported abuses of power as driving motivators in their own, or their loved ones', decision to disaffiliate. Helping families recognize abuses of power can empower them to engage in healthier and more compassionate ways.

Interpersonal Neurobiology

Interpersonal neurobiology (IPNB), with its emphasis on attachment, helps us guide families toward establishing healthy, dynamic relationships that honor differences and similarities, autonomy, and connection. Recognizing chaotic and/or rigid responses and replacing them with more flexible, adaptive, coherent, energized, and stable ones protects family bonds and contributes to individual and relational well-being in the midst of religious difference. Interpersonal integration is the ability to form deep and meaningful connections with others while simultaneously holding onto the unique essence of who we are as individuals (Siegel, 2012). Practicing interpersonal integration by turning kind attention toward others becomes especially relevant in families experiencing religious disaffiliation (Siegel, 2006).

Why Disaffiliate

Reasons for Leaving Faith Community

While reasons for disaffiliation are varied, a significant amount of research indicates that most people who were raised in strongly religious homes leave religion because they no longer believe in some aspect of the supernatural (Altemeyer & Hunsberger, 1997; Hunsberger & Altemeyer, 2006). As skepticism grows, the individual is likely to experience high levels of cognitive dissonance and move toward disaffiliation as a way to resolve those feelings (Krause & Wulff, 2004). Other factors may include political attitudes that diverge from religious ideals, which can predict disaffiliation (Vargas, 2012), and adversity across a variety of contexts, which may cause self-reflection (McMillen, 1999) and realignment of values (Vargas, 2012). Participants interviewed during our research reported four main reasons for disaffiliation (self or family member) from a shared family religion: relational ruptures, hypocritical interactions, intellectual dissonance, and political issues.

Relational Rupture Some participants recounted hurtful interpersonal interactions between themselves (or their family member) and a specific member of religious leadership, the religious congregation, or the family. These relational ruptures seemed to directly contribute to their (or their family member's) decision to no longer participate in the religious community. For some, the rupture occurred through feeling judged and rejected. Ellen (all names are pseudonyms) shared, "the pastor at my home church said I was too young and refused to marry me. So, that was my first, sort of, 'I don't want to be part of this anymore.'" This rejection was the catalyst in a series of painful events which left Ellen no longer wanting to participate in a faith community. Deborah shared a similar experience: The "[Youth Leadership] dumped our family, like completely. They told their kids they couldn't play with, or hang out with, my brothers anymore…because our family was so messed up, which it really wasn't."

Participants also shared relational ruptures around experiences of difference not being accepted. Chris shared, "My dad was and is extremely religious... It has shaped his interactions in the family, I think, in a negative way… His extreme religiosity…[and] justification from the Bible… is divisive." Ellen shared a similar experience related to her own parenting: "As a parent, you can't go where your child is not welcome…I felt like church should have been the place where he was really accepted and supported and where I was accepted and supported, and it was exactly the opposite." Whether from an individual or the church as a whole, relational ruptures between faith communities and families were a significant source of disaffiliation.

Hypocritical Interactions Some participants reported dissonance between the ideals of a connected, caring religious community and what they experienced actually being lived out as contributing to their own or their family member's decision to disaffiliate. "My dad would say he was a real practicing Christian, but a lot of times his behavior was contradictory. So, you kind of get that hypocritical skew," Allison reflected. Deborah used words such as "fake" or "pretending" to describe the experience of hypocritical interactions with both religious family and community members. "It looked like it was so great, from the outside, but really…we all just pretended…No one would have ever known that there were issues."

Intellectual Dissonance For some participants, issues of faith did not stand up to critical questions. Sarah shared that the process of disaffiliating began after "being by myself and independent for the first time and able to just think about a lot of critical questions that I hadn't given myself time to think about." Chris declared, "We need observation, testing, hypothesis testing, theory, to understand the world around us." Some family members could see how the disaffiliated found value in understanding and explaining things intellectually. Sam shared, "He's a very intellectual person. I think he finds a lot of satisfaction and peace in explaining things intellectually." Whether recognized by the affiliated or disaffiliated family member, several participants described this experience of intellectual explanations taking precedence over faith and ultimately being incompatible with previously held religious beliefs.

Political Issues Participants identified three primary political contributors to the decision to disaffiliate from religion: rejection of gay marriage, integration of religion and politics, and 9/11. Matt reflected on the various issues preempting disaffiliation and stated "gay marriage [is] the principal issue that makes me crazy right now." In thinking about religious family and community members, he stated, "their combination of religion and politics is offensive." Religious-based politics and the idea that religion prescribes a certain political agenda were repeated as a cause for disaffiliation. For Tammy, disaffiliation resulted after seeing the destruction of the religious extremists who destroyed the twin towers:

> 9/11 had a huge effect on me spiritually…I realized that people of any religion that are so closed to any other religion are no different than the people who attacked us on 9/11…as long as love is limited and acceptance is limited, then there is no difference, it's just a matter of degree.

Whether due to a relational rupture, hypocritical interactions, intellectual dissonance, or political issues, both the disaffiliated and their affiliated family members reported anywhere from one to three of these reasons as motivating the disaffiliated participant's decision to leave the family-practiced religion.

Process of Disaffiliation: How People Leave

The process of religious disaffiliation seemed to involve both internal and external processes embedded within both a family and larger sociocultural context. We found two distinct continuums of experience: (1) an immediate spiritual disaffiliation to a gradual awareness and (2) indifference to an intense, painful process (Fig. 3.1).

Immediate Spiritual Disaffiliation vs. Gradual Awareness Disaffiliated participants described two very different experiences in terms of how much time they took to leave their family religion. Luke described, "I just stopped going to church," while some participants shared a lengthy process; for example, Tammy reported "It took place over many years." For these participants, leaving sometimes happened more than once. "I have left religion a couple different times actually," Ellen noted. She went on to report that at first, she left because "I got a job, I just worked…and I let that be the reason," suggesting that there were additional reasons. Then, "After I had my son, I tried to go back, I felt like there was some value there for him… I actually tried several different churches and it was that way everywhere."

Indifference vs. Intense, Painful Process Disaffiliated participants described two very different experiences based on the degree of pain related to leaving their family religion. For some this process was emotionally distressing. Tammy described this as:

> A very difficult transition…that took place because of thinking, and growth, and reading, and praying…what I grew up in was so ingrained in me and so important to me as I was growing up, that to leave it was…almost like leaving your family or leaving what is, you know, what's really most important to you.

Participants who shared this painful experience of leaving something so important were in sharp contrast to those who left with indifference rather than pain. Chris reflected, "I just didn't enjoy church at all. I didn't see the point...so I was like, this isn't working."

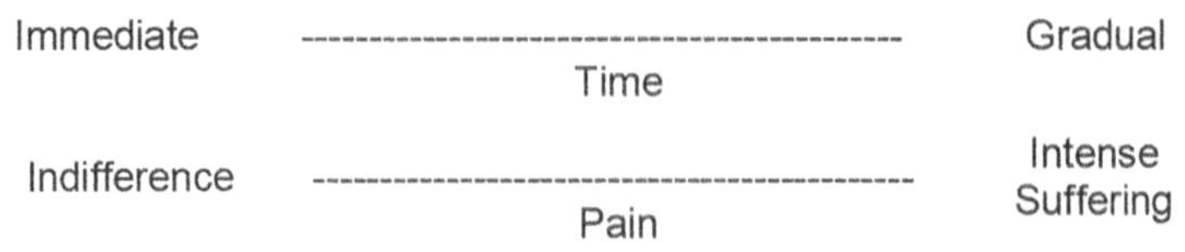

Fig. 3.1 Process of disaffiliation, April Knight

Relational Impact of Disaffiliation

Research indicates that a lack of consensus in religious beliefs and practices can contribute to divisiveness within families (Stokes & Regnerus 2009). Couple relationships are enhanced when both partners hold similar beliefs about the sanctity of their marriage (Lichter & Carmalt, 2009), participate in dyadic spiritual activities (Mahoney et al., 1999), practice the same religion (Myers, 2006), and use personal prayer, reliance on their spiritual community, and beliefs about the sanctification of their marriage toward bolstering their relationship (Mahoney, 2010). Spouses who differ in their church attendance and Biblical interpretations seem more likely to argue, especially about money and housework (Curtis & Ellison, 2002), and tension may arise between interfaith couples when children are born as co-parenting accentuates discrepancies between religious and spiritual values and preferred socialization methods (McCarthy, 2007).

As evidenced by the existing research, families transitioning through a family member's disaffiliation process may feel an acute sense of loss and confusion about how to maintain family bonds within an environment of dissenting opinions about subjects that are sacred to them. In our research, each family system reported experiencing some level of relational distress during the disaffiliation process. Major themes were lack of communication, lack of understanding or feeling "known," lack of participation in family events, and awkward interactions. Many families found ways to navigate differences and come to a place of acceptance.

Lack of Communication The majority of participants talked about difficulty communicating with one another during and post disaffiliation. Disaffiliated family members shared that they did not talk openly about their disaffiliation process with their family members. For some, this was a purposeful decision, and for others it seemed to happen naturally.

Families talked about "walking on eggshells" and not wanting to either offend or be hurt by one another. Some family members limited or shut down communication altogether in order to protect themselves.

Lack of Understanding or Feeling "Known" Families in our study felt a keen sense of loss in not feeling understood or known by one another. Disaffiliated family members reported that their affiliated family members often struggled to recognize the extent to which their religious beliefs impact their worldview and how that view can be quite different from the outside. Affiliated family members described feelings of bewilderment at how this could have happened, confusion, sadness, anger, and varying degrees of rejection.

Lack of Participation in Family Events One of the uniquely challenging aspects of disaffiliation was restructuring family events in ways that did not always center around a common religious foundation. For many, religion provides social resources and places of family connection (Mahoney, 2010) where religious events easily become part of family culture. Families described how challenging it was to find new ways of connecting as a family where each person felt comfortable. Several participants described significant loss as they tried to "go their separate ways" when new common ground couldn't be found.

Awkward Interactions Families in our study described painful, awkward interactions as they relearned how to relate with one another across differences. Many participants were challenged by how to honor their own beliefs and respect the others. They expressed uncertainty about what would offend the other and what might come up in conversation that would offend them. Most expressed some level of tenseness or "walking on eggshells" when engaging with each other across the religious divide.

Acceptance Despite Differences Most families in our study reached a degree of acceptance over the process of disaffiliation and found new ways to connect with one another. For some, this was a long, drawn out process, while for others, it seemed to happen more quickly. Factors that seemed to facilitate this process included family members being able to put their relationships first and finding comfort in seeing disaffiliated family members as happy, peaceful, and contributing members of society.

Understanding the reasons and process of disaffiliation, the relational impact it can have within family systems, and the discrepancies of perspective that are likely to exist will empower clinicians to respond to all family members with empathy and assist them in identifying and implementing new strategies toward protecting family bonds. The case example below illustrates how understanding religious disaffiliation through a family systems, feminist lens can help clinicians guide families toward restructuring their family systems to make space for differing beliefs while retaining family cohesion.

Case Example

Joe and Cathy were a White, middle-class, LDS couple in their mid-40s. Joe was an accountant for a midsize firm and Cathy was a homemaker. They had two sons: their older son, David, was 19 and recently returned home for the summer after completing his freshman year at an out-of-state university, while Caleb, their 16-year-old, was preparing to enter his junior year of high school. Joe and Cathy came to therapy because they were experiencing conflict in their relationship over how to manage a new parenting dilemma. Joe reported, "David has been refusing to go to church with us and is being a bad influence on Caleb." Joe and Cathy disagreed about how to handle the situation. Joe took the stance "our house, our rules" and wanted to lay down an ultimatum. Cathy was reticent to do so, being afraid "it would just push him further away."

Softening Power Differentials and Rigidly Defined Gender Roles

From the onset of my work with the couple, I was aware that power differentials and stereotypic gender roles were likely informing each partner's perspective. My assumption was that each partner likely felt areas of empowerment and disempowerment and that their roles in the relationship could not be untangled from larger social discourses about gender and religion. I began by asking each to describe their roles in the family system, to which Joe described himself as "the provider" and Cathy described herself as "the nurturer." We discussed where these roles originated, and it became clear that they were supported by the family's religious faith that valued fathers' financial provisions for families and women as caretakers at home.

While Joe had significantly more power in a number of ways (financial, decision-making, etc.), he felt inadequate at addressing the more emotional needs of his family. By asking him to reflect on these feelings and begin to notice the impact this was having on his wife, Cathy softened and began to see a more vulnerable side of her partner. We talked about rigid definitions of success, which uncovered further deeper emotion as Joe described his fear of "letting his family down" if he wasn't able to control his children:

> Therapist: So, while you feel pretty confident at work and in your role as the provider for the family, you feel less confident when it comes to working out these differences between you – is that right?
>
> Joe: Yeah… I don't know how to fix this.
>
> Therapist: You're trying – you're trying every way you know how to fix this, but nothing's working. This is not an easy problem… I wonder if there's something you *can* provide for your family right now in the in-between… while you are trying to figure out how to understand and care for each other better.

Joe went on to ask Cathy what she needed from him, and she responded that she needed him to "care when I'm hurting, and to ask me what I think about things and to respect my opinion." These were all things Joe wanted to do for her. As I encouraged Joe to turn toward Cathy in his vulnerability, rather than away from her, Cathy experienced him as more nurturing, and he experienced her as an equal partner. We talked about the way they were "connecting across differences" and how this shifted their perspectives of one another. This led to a further conversation about ways in which they, as parents, could connect with their son, even while he was making choices they wouldn't have wanted for him. By identifying ways in which the larger discourses were positioning family members in opposition to one another, we were able to open up space for Joe and Cathy to make choices that more consistently fit with the values that were religiously supported and central to their lives: loyalty, kindness, patience, and love. It was especially important to counter societal-based power differences by encouraging first Joe to identify his relational desires, take a more vulnerable position, and attune to Cathy (Knudson-Martin, 2013).

Conclusion

When working with families impacted by religious disaffiliation, it is helpful to use a family systems lens that incorporates issues of power and justice within the particular religious cultural context of the family. Useful therapist interventions may include (1) helping family members feel heard and understood in their unique experiences, which may result in more curiosity and less fear, processing emotions in the context of religious beliefs, (2) helping families identify and emphasize relational values over power and control values, (3) working with families to enhance distress tolerance for different religious beliefs, (4) bolstering effective communication through shared family moral (not religious) values, and (5) protecting family bonds through negotiating new rituals.

Religious disaffiliation impacts full family systems. While working with families through these transitions is challenging, it also provides an opportunity to help family members find hope and reconnection in ways that include and support all voices. Therapists working with families through these processes should be mindful of the ways religion can be a helpful resource in these skills, as well as ways in which it may be potentially limiting or harmful to family relationships. Families who have the support to practice the skills outlined above may be empowered to prevent relational wounds, expedite healing processes, protect family bonds across differences, and explore relational possibilities previously masked by narrow or rigid ways of experiencing religious and spiritual values (see Esmiol Wilson, 2018).

References

Altemeyer, B., & Hunsberger, B. (1997). *Amazing conversions: Why some turn to faith and others abandon religion*. Amherst, NY: Prometheus Books.

Beder, J. (2004). Loss of the assumptive world: How we deal with death and loss. *Omega, 50*(4), 255–265.

Curtis, K. T., & Ellison, C. G. (2002). Religious heterogamy and marital conflict: Findings from the National Survey of Families and Households. *Journal of Family Issues, 23*(4), 551–576.

Esmiol Wilson, E. (2018). From assessment to activism: Utilizing a justice-informed framework to guide spiritual and religious clinical interventions. In E. Esmiol Wilson & L. A. Nice (Eds.), *Socially just religious and spiritual interventions: Ethical uses of therapeutic power, AFTA Springer Briefs*. Cham, Switzerland: Springer.

Fisher, A. R. (2016). A review and conceptual model of the research on doubt, disaffiliation, and related religious changes. *Psychology of Religion and Spirituality*. Advance online publication, 1–10, https://doi.org/10.1037/rel0000088

Hunsberger, B., & Altemeyer, B. (2006). *Atheists: A groundbreaking study of America's nonbelievers*. Amherst, NY: Prometheus Books.

Knudson-Martin, C. (2013). Why power matters: Creating a foundation for mutual support in couple therapy. *Family Process, 52*, 5–18.

Kosmin, B. A., & Keysar, A. (2009). American nones: the profile of the no religion population. In *In American religious identification survey*. Hartford, CT: Trinity College.

Krause, N., & Wulff, K. (2004). Religious doubt and health: Exploring the potential dark side of religion. *Sociology of Religion, 65*(1), 35–56.
Lichter, D. T., & Carmalt, J. H. (2009). Religion and marital quality in low-income couples. *Social Science Review, 38*(1), 168–187.
Mahoney, A. (2010). Religion in families 1999 to 2009: A relational spirituality framework. *Journal of Marriage and the Family, 72*(4), 805–827. https://doi.org/10.1111/j.1741-3737.2010.00732.x
Mahoney, A., Pargament, K. I., Jewell, T., Swank, A. B., Scott, E., Emery, E., et al. (1999). Marriage and the spiritual realm: The role of proximal and distal religious constructs in marital functioning. *Journal of Family Psychology, 13*(3), 321–338.
McCarthy, K. (2007). Pluralist family values: Domestic strategies for living with religious difference. *Annals of the American Academy of Political and Social Science, 612*, 188–208.
McMillen, J. C. (1999). Better for it: How people benefit from adversity. *Social Work, 44*(5), 455–468.
Myers, S. M. (2006). Religious homogamy and marital quality: Historical and generational patterns, 1980–1997. *Journal of Marriage and Family, 68*(2), 292–304.
Siegel, D. J. (2006). An interpersonal neurobiology approach to psychotherapy. *Psychiatric Annals, 36*(4), 248–256.
Siegel, D. J. (2012). *The developing mind, second edition: How relationships and the brain interact to shape who we are*. New York: Guilford Press.
Smith, T.W., Marsden, P., Hout, M., & Kim, J. (2011). General social surveys, 2010. *National Opinion Research Center: The Roper Center for Public Opinion Research*, University of Connecticut.
Stokes, C. E., & Regnerus, M. D. (2009). When faith divides family: Religious discord and adolescent reports of parent-child relations. *Social Science Research, 38*, 155–167.
Vargas, N. (2012). Retrospective accounts of religious disaffiliation in the United States: Stressors, skepticism, and political factors. *Sociology of Religion, 73*(2), 200–223. https://doi.org/10.1093/socrel/srr044
Winell, M. (2007). *Leaving the fold*. Berkeley, CA: Apocryphile Press.

Chapter 4
Colliding Discourses: Families Negotiating Religion, Sexuality, and Identity

Justine D'Arrigo-Patrick, Elizabeth D'Arrigo-Patrick, and Chris Hoff

Positioning ideas, values, and experiences as disparate is a common practice within Western individualism, and all too often this oppositionality creates either/or systems of thinking that limit our options to two extremes (Keating, 2012). We are easily seduced into seeing realities as dichotomous or differing views as inherently oppositional. The effects of this are vast and contribute to people becoming alienated from relationship, from hopes they hold for their lives, and from communities that once provided meaning and support. The intersection of religion and sexual orientation is a site where these effects have had great consequence for lesbian, gay, and bisexual (LGB) persons (Barton, 2010; Ryan, Huebner, Diaz, & Sanchez, 2009).

For LGB persons raised within faith communities, it is often difficult to navigate how to reconcile one's faith with one's sexual orientation (Levy & Edmiston, 2014; Shuck & Liddle, 2001; Walker, 2013). This remains true even though there is increased visibility, legal protections, and federal rights for LGB persons today. The reality is many still face potential losses within their family and faith community as a result of living authentically.

Navigating faith and sexual orientation is not just tricky within faith communities but can be difficult within the LGBTQI+ community as well (Buchanan, Dzelme, Harris, & Hecker, 2001). LGB persons of faith may experience a lack of understanding about their faith identity from the broader LGBTQI+ community who may also see religion and sexual orientation in disparate ways. For the LGBTQI+ community, religion has often represented oppressive and dehumanizing beliefs and practices that have been a source of personal and communal degradation (Barton, 2010; Buchanan et al., 2001), making it something many

J. D'Arrigo-Patrick (✉) · E. D'Arrigo-Patrick · C. Hoff
California State University, San Bernardino, CA, USA
e-mail: Justine.darrigopatrick@csusb.edu

E. Esmiol Wilson, L. Nice (eds.), *Socially Just Religious and Spiritual Interventions*, AFTA SpringerBriefs in Family Therapy, https://doi.org/10.1007/978-3-030-01986-0_4

LGB persons must insulate from. Thus, LGB persons who want to maintain connection with their faith often feel caught between community and identity. On the one hand, they experience rejection in their faith community for their sexual orientation and, in return, experience confusion and/or exasperation from the LGBTQI+ community for holding onto a faith identity within a community that has rejected them. This produces a complex web for religious LGB persons to navigate.

While there is growing visibility of LGB individuals who are creating intentional communities of faith where they can live in the both/and, progress has been slow, and there continues to be no shortage of negative views of the other from both sides. We see this continued chasm as the direct result of the oppositional ways in which we position ideas as disparate (McGeorge, Carlson, & Toomey, 2014). Positioning ideas in disparate ways not only presents LGB persons with challenges in living in the both/and, but it can force conservative Christian families of LGB persons into making either/or decisions about how to negotiate life with their LGB family member. Some families get captured by the idea that they must denounce their faith for the sake of maintaining connection with their LGB family member, while others get stuck in the idea that they must maintain their religious and spiritual allegiances above all else, thereby losing connection with or rejecting their LGB family member. It is our position that this either/or choice is an unnecessary one, produced within a context of power that dictates acceptable ways of living and restricts identity options. Within this larger context of power, we conceptualize heteronormative and homophobic discourses as creating conditions where families feel left with little choice, inciting decisions that might be against their better judgments or even perhaps their preferences, hopes, and dreams for how to do family. Therefore, we are interested in intentionally critiquing the ways religion and sexual orientation get situated as opposing within our cultural narratives. We are also interested in highlighting ways that we believe families can create paths forward that allow them to maintain meaningful connection to one another and to a religious faith that has served as a foundation of the family in connecting it with a larger community.

Social Location of Authors

As authors, we come to writing this chapter and to this clinical practice with a range of experiences, identities, and religious/spiritual practices. Justine identifies as gender-queer and queer. Elizabeth identifies as a lesbian cisgender female. Chris identifies as a heterosexual cisgender male. Justine and Elizabeth attend a United Church of Christ church, and both grew up under the influence of evangelical Christianity. Chris was raised under Roman Catholic traditions and has since converted to Zen Buddhism. We also share several similarities, in that we all identify as White and attended the same Master's and Doctorate programs in marital and family therapy, and each practices from a postmodern, poststructural, and collaborative therapeutic framework. Our combined work with LGBTQ individuals and families, and personal experiences (JDP and EDP) navigating religious and LGBTQ identities, has led us to orient ourselves to this current clinical practice model with much thought and intention.

Theoretical Orientation

This work was guided conceptually by post-oppositional thought (Keating, 2012), relational interviewing (Madigan, 2017; Zucker, 2015), and an activism through collaborating framework (D'Arrigo-Patrick, Hoff, Knudson-Martin, & Tuttle, 2017).

One of the central premises of post-oppositional practice allows for holding contradictory ideas in one space, without the need to situate one position over another even if such a position aligns best with our own personal and philosophical positions (Bhattacharya, 2016). Situating the work with a post-oppositional lens draws us into intentionally holding space for commonalities that exist within perceived contradictions. Some additional post-oppositional traits (Keating, 2018) that guided our work include a desire to be entirely (at times paradoxically) inclusive: to seek and create complex commonalities and alliances for change; an acknowledgment (and, whenever possible, acceptance) of paradox, contradiction, multiplicity, and intellectual humility; an open-minded, optimistic, flexible approach to thinking that entails self-reflection and acknowledges limitations, uncertainty, and the possibility of error; and finally, the presupposition that guilt and blame are not useful but accountability is.

Relational interviewing aligns with our post-oppositional stance as it abandons a focus on the individuals in the conflict and instead makes inquiries on what made up the "moral character" of the relationship prior to the onset of current conflict or problems (Madigan, 2017). A relational interviewing stance positions the therapist to better understand the dilemma, dreams, hopes, and ambitions of a family, what's obscuring them from getting what they want while circumventing individual blame and debate through the use of externalizing language (Zucker, 2015).

Therapists who embrace the activism through collaborating framework (D'Arrigo-Patrick et al., 2017) challenge dominant practices by refraining from social education and consciousness raising, ultimately foregrounding their relational lens, and are very careful not to use the power inherent in the therapist role to impose or colonize. This means that while we may have many experiences where religion creates challenges for acceptance and affirmation, we do not see it as an inevitable reality that the family needs to be made aware of in order to overcome. Instead, we hold this as just one of many possibilities for how religion and sexuality intersect, which leaves open the possibility to situate religion as a foundation for affirmation and acceptance.

Religion as a Site of Oppressive Dichotomies

Religious Messages for Families

Within evangelical Christianity, which is where we focus our discussion, there are deeply ingrained beliefs and enduring messages that are used to counsel families of LGB persons to encourage, and many times even require, LGB members to reject, suppress, and/or change their same-sex orientation. These messages are influenced by the belief that sexual orientation is a choice or a behavior that can be altered (Morrow & Beckstead, 2004; O'Brien, 2004; Walker, 2013). In this case, same-sex orientation is seen as an immoral desire of the flesh or sinful temptation that one must resist and repent from. This produces a context where LGB persons' commitment to faith and God is put to the test. Families become enlisted to intercede on behalf of the LGB family member, which is sometimes spoken about as "praying the gay away," or "tough love" in which LGB persons are required to change in order to be accepted. In many ways, these responses become storied within evangelical communities as the ultimate loving act toward the LGB family member. It becomes understood as love through the idea that truly loving others, in this case their family member, is to hold them accountable to "holy" ways of living that support intimacy with God. And because an LGB identity is seen as sinful, i.e., a state of living that would separate them from God, loved ones must not give them the message that this part of their identity or life is acceptable.

Reparative Therapy

Perhaps one of the most blatant ways these messages and beliefs have taken on force in the lives of LGB people and their families is through the "reparative" therapy movement. As alluded to above, the central message within "reparative" therapy (Serovich, Grafsky, & Gangamma, 2012) is that it is possible for people to change their sexual or affectional orientation. Proponents of "reparative" therapy would argue that possibility for change in orientation ultimately comes down to how committed LGB persons are to their relationship with God above self. For the most part, "reparative" therapy has been the only offering within evangelical Christianity for how families can and ought to respond to their LGB family member (Walker, 2013). As a result, families' options for building relationships with both LGB family members and faith communities that create space for sexual identity and faith identities to exist in harmony are severely limited. The effect on families is that they may be faced with difficult choices about whether to turn their LGB family member away or to themselves walk away from a community of support and meaning.

Therapy as Reinforcing Oppressive Dichotomies

Therapeutic Messages for LGB Persons

Within therapeutic communities, we often conceptualize LGB persons coming from Christian evangelical contexts as having endured spiritual abuse (Barton, 2010; Bowland, Foster, & Vosler, 2013; Super & Jacobson, 2011) and approach clinical work from a framework of trauma. Much of the therapeutic work then focuses on assisting LGB people in separating from what are seen as damaging and oppressive ideologies, beliefs, and messages that become internalized over time and get in the way of embracing one's sexual orientation (Barton; Yarhouse, 2008). From this stance, religious beliefs are positioned as impediments to self-acceptance, and the process of deconstructing them critically is privileged.

Therapeutic Messages for Families

We would say the same holds true when working with families of LGB persons (LaSala, 2010). Therapeutic conversations often get centered around what is more valuable, connection and relationship with their family member or membership in their faith community (Bowland et al., 2013), reifying the perspective that either/or is the only way. In other words, it has been a commonplace to help families let go of the harmful beliefs they have been "indoctrinated" with so that they are able to accept their LGB family member (Martin, Hutson, Kazyak, & Scherrer, 2010). As a result, therapeutic conversations often focus more around how to accept their LGB family member despite their religious beliefs. These conversations may focus less on how to offer acceptance and affirmation of the LGB family member in ways that are made possible by their religious beliefs. In other words, we do not typically think of families loving and affirming their LGB family member because of their religion, but rather, in spite of their religion.

Therapeutic Messages on Scripture

Another more recent message from LGB affirmative psychotherapy literature (Bowland et al., 2013) and gay Christian activists is that LGB persons and families need to adapt their reading and understanding of biblical text and teachings from a literal interpretation to a contextual and historical interpretation. In fact, this is described as one of the foundational processes for LGB identity integration and family acceptance (Beckstead, 2012). Families are invited to learn varying theological perspectives about biblical texts most often used against same-sex orientation. In doing so, LGB persons and their families can reinterpret the foundations of their Christian beliefs in a way that makes space for integrating LGB identity and Christian identity. This process has been described as useful and even essential in supporting LGB persons to integrate their faith identity and LGB identity (Borgman, 2009). Yet these messages perpetuate a dichotomous view that literal versus contextual interpretations are inherently oppositional.

Religion as Relational Invitation

Rather than remaining captured by the limiting narrative that conservative Christian beliefs are in opposition of accepting an LGB family member, we see Christian values of love, compassion, family steadfastness, and justice to be central components in supporting families on their journeys through coming out experiences. The value of love is demonstrated through a number of active exchanges: God is love (e.g., 1 John 4:8), loving God (e.g., John 15:9), being loved by God (e.g., 1 Corinthians 13:1–13), loving neighbors (e.g., Mark 12:31; Colossians 3:14), and loving our enemies (e.g., Matthew 5:43–48). Compassion for self and others is demonstrated through scriptures and teachings that emphasize caring relationships and loving others as ourselves (e.g., John 13:35). The value of justice supports processes that turn our eyes toward people on the margins of society (e.g., Deuteronomy 10:18; Psalm 140:12; Psalm 146:7–9; Job 34:18–19; Micah 6:8). The emphasis here is that all people matter to God, and all people (no matter how unclean they are deemed by the culture of religion) are a part of the body of Christ, carrying out a valuable part of the human family, and every person is made in the image of God.

It is our position that there is room to see a family's religious beliefs as being the site of acceptance and affirmation rather than a barrier that makes acceptance and affirmation difficult. In working with families of an LGB person, it is important to shift our lens away from assisting families to cast off harmful religious teachings and learn to accept their LGB family member in spite of their religion. The teachings of love, compassion, and justice serve as a beautiful invitation to many families for how they can draw upon their religious values to support them in coming to accept their LGB family member. The difference this creates in orienting toward families' religious beliefs as supports rather than constraints is that families are presented with an open invitation to relationship rather than an either/or choice of having to decide what to keep and what to leave behind and whether that be one's LGB family member or deeply held religious teachings. In the same way, LGB people may not feel constrained to rejecting their faith and family if their religious values were understood in ways that support love, compassion, justice, and authentic living.

Case Application

The Family

I (Chris) was meeting with parents Steven, Michele, and their 17-year-old son James who had all recently returned to the United States from Africa where they had been doing missionary work for several years. They had been referred to me by a local university on account of concerns about their only son who had recently come out to them. This news was quite disturbing to the parents because if his sexual orientation became known among their evangelical community, it could have devastating effects on their missionary work and their livelihoods. The experience was equally as difficult for the son who was facing challenges in his schooling and was experiencing what he described as severe depression, with one suicide attempt while still in Africa. This suicide attempt by James precipitated the family's return home to the United States and their decision to seek help.

Instead of focusing on the individuals in the conflicted family relationship, I asked them about the "moral character" of the family prior to James coming out. In this way, I tried to partner with the spiritual and religious foundation the family valued. This approach asks about the relational ethics, values, and preferred moral principles of the family, eliciting the ways their evangelical beliefs and teachings support these places. This use of relational interviewing (Madigan, 2017; Zucker, 2015) is to circumvent practices of the conflict (shame, blame, accusation, anger) that holds families frozen within the difficulties that we might often conceptualize as being produced by oppressive religious ideologies. This shift invites us to begin the session with "re-moralizing" dialogues that help families rediscover ethics, values, and principles once important to the family's ethical story (Madigan). These values and principles may, in part, emerge from the family's commitment to living in ways that reflect the "teachings of scripture" that center love, compassion, and steadfastness to the family.

Questions for the Family

The following are examples of some questions I used to support the relational interviewing approach and generate reflections within the family that stood alongside their religious beliefs. These sorts of questions helped me begin to understand the family's dilemma, dreams, hopes, and what are they trying to achieve, and find out their intentions and their experience of what's obscuring them from getting what they want (Zucker, 2015).

- What is the dream of this family?
- What does the relationship need right now to achieve its dreams?
- What is obscuring the intentions of the family – getting in the way of what it wants?

- What tasks or actions does this family need from you now?
- What has the family lost that it needs now?
- What has injured the family?
- What abilities have slipped away?
- What gives you hope you can give the family relationship what it is asking for?
- How is the family still important to you despite this struggle?
- What about this family has withstood the struggle?
- What ways do you call forward the teachings of your faith to support the dream of this family?

These sorts of questions led to the naming of an anchoring metaphor based on the ethics, values, and principles of the family which the family described as family unity. This anchoring metaphor was quite helpful in this case, and I returned to the anchoring metaphor time and time again whenever conversations became difficult or "stuck." This ethic and value of family unity was supported, in part, by what the family honored in their religious and spiritual practice, making it possible to bolster this religious commitment to serve as part of the foundation for the work. This produced an alternative way for me to invite beliefs forward, rather than having to sideline or overcome them.

Clinical Interventions

Religious Assessment

Early in the work, it was important to me to determine what role the family's conservative Christian beliefs would play, and as to be expected, it was complex. In the beginning, Steven shared that he and his wife were "far apart on what we could live with" in relation to James' sexuality, but he also spoke of the intention to "learn to live in disagreement." I sought further understanding of this intention in order to connect it to Steven and Michele's parental values, asking "What values support this intention?" At the same time, James spoke of his intention to stay involved in the family's faith community. He still considered himself a Christian but was feeling "the pressure" of hiding his identity and spoke of experiencing "oppression" and "control" from his parents.

On the same hand, the family's Christian beliefs, faith, and community engagement provided fertile ground for the development of "re-moralizing" dialogues that supported and sustained the family throughout this difficult transition. For example, Steven, early in the work, spoke of love for his family and son trumping all other considerations and linked this love to his Christian faith. And the whole family spoke often of how their faith was a source of agency in the face of fear and what often could be paralyzing uncertainty. On the continuum of religious assessment (Esmiol Wilson, 2018), this family seemed to lean more toward the relational, loving, and hopeful end of the spectrum, demonstrated by their steadfast commitment to learning about one another and remaining open to exploring their family "road map."

Space to Counter and Collaborate

It would be easy at this point for a therapist to step in and work with the family toward a goal of casting off harmful religious teachings and learning to accept their LGB family member in spite of their religion. However, externalizing and naming the rediscovered ethics, values, and principles, often grounded in the family's Christian faith, helped me support the family's "re-moralizing" counter-narratives that developed and strengthened throughout the case. My willingness to hold the complexity, even when family members would retreat to unhelpful positions that had them moving further away rather than closer together, also proved quite helpful as time progressed. One scenario presented itself as particularly crucial early on in the work where I simultaneously balanced countering and collaborating positions with the family. The parents continually storied their son's sexual orientation as a "phase" and as something that could be eventually changed. I considered that such a position may have been influenced by oppressive religious and social discourses, although I did not insist that the parents shift to this belief or word choice. Instead, I made explicit that I believed it was important to be affirmative of James' sexual orientation and that going forward I would be using language that more accurately reflected my affirming position and James' preference while at the same time accepting the parent's perspectives.

Activism Through Collaborating

To help detail how I assessed what was helpful and what was problematic about their religious beliefs, and how I countered or collaborated, or worked with complexity, it is important to highlight D'Arrigo-Patrick, Hoff, Knudson-Martin, and Tuttle's (2017) activism through collaborating framework. Aspects of this framework include the following:

Caution Regarding Social Education During this case, I was very hesitant and cautious regarding social education. I knew that the common course could easily lead to the position critiqued earlier of attempting to influence the family into casting off harmful religious teachings and learning to accept their LGB family member in spite of their religion. I believe social education, or what Bruno LaTour (2005) calls instant sociology, replicates the same colonizing processes we often critique in family therapy. In order to remain accountable to the desire to refrain from imposing or knowing better, I was intentional in keeping curiosity about the dream of the family centered in the work and took care to privilege the family's leading.

Privileging Client Lead Throughout the case, I privileged client lead in a number of ways, adhering to an overall ethical responsibility to the clients and their sense of personal agency, which aligns closely with activism through collaborating. I would bring critical ideas into the therapeutic conversation when appropriate, but I would do so in a very tentative fashion, in an attempt to be mindful of therapist power. This was typically done in the effort of transparency, often borrowing from Harlene Anderson's (2006) work on making my private thoughts public which is grounded in relational understanding (Bahktin, 1986).

Utilizing Deconstruction Using deconstruction in therapy (Carey, Walther, & Russell, 2009) allowed me to ask about taken-for-granted ideas or dominant discourses, in and around their faith, that might or might not be helpful to the family at this particular time. This process provided lines of inquiry that developed ways of inverting "binary opposition" in order to make visible marginalized meanings, stories of preference, and wider spaces of possibility. An important point of emphasis here is that deconstruction, in this case, was not used to directly take apart what could have been seen as the family's oppressive beliefs. Rather I accessed deconstruction as a way to pose wonderings about how the family saw various beliefs and ideas, not just religious ones, as having an impact on their lives as a family.

Considerations for the Therapist

It is important for affirmative therapists to have an understanding of the impacts of heterosexism on the mental health of LGB individuals and to know that evangelical Christianity often marginalizes LGB individuals based on a set of beliefs and assumptions that heterosexuality is the only valid way of living and, therefore, the preferred norm (McGeorge & Carlson, 2011). I was also interested in using my power in ways that challenged these sorts of assumptions, made visible dominant discourse, and questioned taken-for-granted norms, in an effort to take a political stand against the oppressive influences that impact clients' lives (White & Epston, 1990). In these efforts, I found it helpful to hold several considerations close that provided the ground for various lines of inquiry. These considerations in this case included:

- How do we create space to redefine what it means to love this child?
- What will be the social cost of loving this child?
- What does sexuality mean now?
- When supported, what might that mean for this child's psychic energy? (school, depression, etc.)
- How are this family's problems located in society and culture?
- Is this going faster than the parents are comfortable with?
- What does it mean to be parents of a gay child?

These sorts of considerations led to the naming of another anchoring metaphor based on the intentions of the parents and the child, which the family described as a road map. This road map of coming out for James was consistently returned to and often renegotiated throughout the case. There were times the road map was moving too slowly (for James) or too fast (for Michele), but it often provided a rich, jumping off place for other conversations closely linked to the road map. Some examples of these conversations included a several-session conversation around stigma and its effects on Michele leading to her questioning, "how do I do it?" For example, how she might function in the face of stigma and its effects, and conversations with the family around "safe spaces" and who might be helpful and supportive to them in this transition.

Conclusion

At the time of this writing, the family has traveled far down their particular road map. Some of the parent's worst fears did come to pass as they moved further down the map, and James' sexuality became more known. They lost one large donor that had supported their missionary efforts and experienced cutoff from an important family member. However, there were many surprises along the way. The parents did disclose to the head Pastor of their home church and were met with acceptance and understanding. After the disclosure, they were also asked to take a leadership role in the church's family ministry. These sorts of developments, and there were several, even surprised me (Chris).

We understand that more explicitly activist affirmative therapists may find much to critique in our approach. However, we believe that our relational interviewing (Madigan, 2017; Zucker, 2015) and post-oppositional (Keating, 2012) stance, grounded in an activism through collaborating framework (D'Arrigo-Patrick et al., 2017), created a therapeutic ground that reduced binary opposition, held complexity, and embraced uncertainty all while partnering with the family's religion.

In this approach overall, we closely align with queer theory icon Judith Butler's (MacLeod, 2016) recent work that invites us to be more interested in coalitions and alliances in order to support the coming together of groups who identify with very different kinds of issues. We see value in backgrounding identity claims that create dichotomies (e.g., LGB vs. Christian) for the purposes of a common struggle (e.g., family unity), thereby creating opportunities for generative alliances to be developed. What we hope we have offered here is at least one version of how this kind of articulating together can be made possible within contexts where either/or stances typically dominate.

References

Anderson, H. (2006). Dialogue: Appreciating the possibilities inherent in it. In S. McNamee & H. Anderson (Guest Eds.). *AI practitioner: International journal of AI best practices. Expanding organizational practices: Lessons from therapeutic conversations* (pp. 9–11). August 2006, London.

Bakhtin, M. (1986). *Speech, genre and other late essays* (trans: W. McGee). Austin, TX: University of Texas Press.

Barton, B. (2010). "Abomination": Life as a Bible belt gay. *Journal of Homosexuality, 57*(4), 465–484.

Beckstead, A. L. (2012). Can we change sexual orientation? *Archives of Sexual Behavior, 41*, 121–134.
Bhattacharya, K. (2016). Dropping my anchor here: A post-oppositional approach to social justice work in education. *Critical Questions in Education, 7*(3), 197–214.
Borgman, A. L. (2009). LGB allies and Christian identity: A qualitative exploration of resolving conflicts and integrating identities. *Journal of Counseling Psychology, 56*(4), 508.
Bowland, S. E., Foster, K., & Vosler, A. N. R. (2013). Culturally competent and spiritually sensitive therapy with lesbian and gay Christians. *Social Work, 58*(4), 321–332.
Buchanan, M., Dzelme, K., Harris, D., & Hecker, L. (2001). Challenges of being simultaneously gay or lesbian and spiritual and/or religious: A narrative perspective. *The American Journal of Family Therapy, 29*, 435–449.
Carey, M., Walther, S., & Russell, S. (2009). The absent but implicit: A map to support therapeutic enquiry. *Family Process, 48*(3), 319–331.
D'Arrigo-Patrick, J., Hoff, C., Knudson-Martin, C., & Tuttle, A. (2017). Navigating critical theory and postmodernism: Social justice and therapist power in family therapy. *Family Process, 56*(3), 574–588.
Esmiol Wilson, E. (2018). From assessment to activism: Utilizing a justice-informed framework to guide spiritual and religious clinical interventions. In E. Esmiol Wilson & L. A. Nice (Eds.), *Socially just religious and spiritual interventions: Ethical uses of therapeutic power, AFTA Springer Briefs*. Cham, Switzerland: Springer.
Keating, A. (2012). *Transformation now!: Toward a post-oppositional politics of change*. Chicago: University of Illinois Press.
Keating, A. (2018). *Invitation to post-oppositional practice.* Keynote presented at the American Family Therapy Practice, Austin, TX.
LaSala, M. C. (2010). *Coming out, coming home: Helping families adjust to a gay or lesbian child.* New York: Columbia University Press.
Latour, B. (2005). *Reassembling the social: An introduction to actor-network-theory (Clarendon lectures in management studies).* Oxford, NY: Oxford University Press.
Levy, D. L., & Edmiston, A. (2014). Sexual identity, gender identity and a Christian upbringing: Comparing two studies. *Journal of Women and Social Work, 29*(1), 66–77.
MacLeod, S. (2016). Global trouble: American philosopher Judith Butler discusses American vulgarity, middle east upheaval, and other forms of the global crisis. *The Cairo Review of Global Affairs.*
Madigan, S. (2017). Narrative therapy-informed relational interviewing – emotionally preparing conflicted couple relationships for possible re-unification, separation, mediation, and family courtrooms. *Nordic Family Therapy Journal, 45*, 138–158.
Martin, K. A., Hutson, D. J., Kazyak, E., & Scherrer, K. S. (2010). Advice with children come out: The cultural "tool kits" of parents. *Journal of Family Issues, 31*(7), 960–991.
McGeorge, C., & Carlson, T. (2011). Deconstructing heterosexism: Becoming an LGB affirmative heterosexual couple and family therapist. *Journal of Marital and Family Therapy, 37*(1), 14–26.
McGeorge, C. R., Carlson, T. S., & Toomey, R. B. (2014). The intersection of spirituality, religion, sexual orientation, and gender identity in family therapy training: An exploration of student's beliefs and practices. *Contemporary Family Therapy, 36*, 497–506.
Morrow, S. L., & Beckstead, A. L. (2004). Conversion therapies for same-sex attracted clients in religious conflict: Context, predisposing factors, experiences, and implications for therapy. *The Counseling Psychologist, 32*(5), 641–650.
O'Brien, J. (2004). Wrestling the angel of contradiction: Queer Christian identities. *Culture and Religion, 5*(2), 179–202.
Ryan, C., Huebner, D., Diaz, R. M., & Sanchez, J. (2009). Family rejection as a predictor of negative health outcomes in white and Latino lesbian, gay and bisexual young adults. *Pediatrics, 123*(1), 346–352.

Serovich, J. M., Grafsky, E. L., & Gangamma, R. (2012). Research on reorientation therapy. In J. J. Bigner & J. L. Wetchler (Eds.), *Handbook of LGBT-affirmative couple and family therapy* (pp. 433–441). New York: Routledge.

Shuck, K. D., & Liddle, B. J. (2001). Religious conflicts experienced by lesbian, gay, and bisexual individuals. *Journal of Gay & Lesbian Psychotherapy, 5*(2), 63–82.

Super, J., & Jacobson, L. (2011). Religious abuse: Implications for counseling lesbian, gay, bisexual, and transgender individuals. *Journal of LGBT Issues in Counseling, 5*(3–4), 180–196.

Walker, M. D. (2013). When clients want your help to 'Pray away the gay': Implications for couple and family therapists. *Journal of Feminist Family Therapy, 25*, 112–134.

White, M., & Epston, D. (1990). *Narrative means to therapeutic ends*. New York: WW Norton & Company.

Yarhouse, M. (2008). Narrative sexual identity therapy. *American Journal of Family Therapy, 36*(3), 196–210.

Zucker, L. (2015). *Escaping blame in couples therapy*. Workshop presented at the Los Angeles Postmodern Therapy Gathering, Los Angeles, CA.

Chapter 5
Before You Were Born I Consecrated You (Jeremiah 1:5, NRSV): Spiritual Resilience and Resistance Within Transgender Families and Communities

Elijah C. Nealy

Coming out as transgender requires tremendous internal energy and courage. Despite progress made, transgender and gender diverse people continue to face high rates of harassment, discrimination, and violence (James et al., 2016). At the same time, resistance in the form of naming and maintaining one's own sense of identity in the face of persistent and pervasive invisibility and oppression can both elicit and amplify inner strength and resilience (Singh, Hays, & Watson, 2011).

Part of societal stigma emerges from the general public's lack of familiarity with trans people and the continued diagnosis of gender dysphoria as a psychiatric illness. However, much ongoing stigma remains rooted in historical and present-day negative religious beliefs about trans and gender diverse people (Mann, 2013; Tanis, 2003).

These messages, alongside experiences of rejection and discrimination, place transgender people at high risk for a poor sense of self and self-esteem, self-harm, and harassment and violence from others. It is essential that family therapists and other clinicians engage trans clients in not only navigating external discrimination but also dismantling the effects of internalized negative religious beliefs and practices. In this chapter I will explore the impact of such religious messages on the identity of transgender people, share my clinical framework, and offer spiritually integrative clinical interventions for working with trans clients. I will also share a case study to illustrate the role that resistance and resilience play in healing internalized religious shame within transgender families.

E. C. Nealy (✉)
Department of Social Work and Equitable Community Practice, University of Saint Joseph, West Hartford, CT, USA
e-mail: enealy@usj.edu

E. Esmiol Wilson, L. Nice (eds.), *Socially Just Religious and Spiritual Interventions*, AFTA SpringerBriefs in Family Therapy, https://doi.org/10.1007/978-3-030-01986-0_5

Negative Religious Messages and Transgender Identity

Within many faith communities, transgender individuals have historically been viewed as sinful, sick (mental illness), perverted, even dangerous, and violent. As a result, transgender people have often had to choose between being their authentic selves and being excluded or disaffiliated from their faith communities (Mollenkott & Sheridan, 2010).

Negative religious messages about transgender people are communicated verbally and behaviorally, for example, insisting on a binary gender construct as "God's will," teaching that being transgender is a sin, or excluding transgender and gender diverse people from their faith community because they are "living in sin" (Mollenkott, 2001).

While a growing number of faith communities have become more open and affirming of trans and gender diverse individuals, even nonreligious trans individuals cannot escape hearing religious shame and stigma about trans and gender diverse individuals though radio, TV, print media, online blogs, social media outlets, and casual conversations. As a result, much stigma (external and internalized) and concomitant discrimination and violence remain rooted in religious interpretations that view transgender identities as sinful.

My Social Location

Given my belief that therapists are not neutral, I want to begin by naming the aspects of my social location that shape and impact my clinical practice and social justice work. I am a white transgender man who spent my formative years growing up as a girl-child within a fundamentalist Baptist faith community in a blue-collar neighborhood. It was the 1970s. No one talked about gender identity or transgender people. There were no visible transgender role models, no transgender talk shows, and definitely no media stories about transgender teenagers.

Within the context of that faith environment, there was no place to acknowledge my authentic self. I knew implicitly I dared not speak my truth out loud. I knew the survival of my genderqueer body self-demanded silence. By the age of 12, I was depressed and actively suicidal.

Religious Messages of Gender Binarism

Most fundamentalist religious contexts (Catholic, Protestant, Jewish, Muslim, etc.) believe there are only two sexes/genders: male and female. There are no other options, nothing in-between male and female. In this framework, transgender identities do not exist.

Claiming to be transgender, or transitioning to live in a gender other than the sex assigned at birth, is viewed as a violation of God's will, an abomination to God, and a rejection of who God created you to be (your sex assigned at birth). Living in your affirmed gender is a sin, so therefore being your authentic self is a sin.

Your only choice to live in "right relationship" with God and your faith community is to deny your authentic gender identity and develop a false self that matches the sex you were assigned at birth. If you refuse to follow these understandings of sex/gender or these interpretations of sacred texts, trans people are typically rejected and ostracized.

For trans people growing up in these environments, it is virtually impossible not to internalize at least some of these negative messages about their value and worth, their ability to be connected to the Sacred/Divine, or their right to participate in intimate relationships, friendships, and faith communities.

Religious Messages of Shame and Denial of Self

Internalizing shaming religious beliefs about your identity can lead to both pervasive and long-lasting effects. For example, if your faith community does not believe transgender identity exists, this sends a message that you do not really exist. This often necessitates dissociation from self – mentally, emotionally, physically, and sexually. Denial of one's spiritual self, and/or transgender self, may become necessary as a protective factor. As inauthenticity becomes essential to survival, the false self frequently becomes a way of life.

Internalizing messages that one's identity is wrong, sinful, and unlovable often leads to deeply embedded shame and self-hatred. This can contribute to depression and hopelessness or anger and rage at self, others, or the Divine. Despair about oneself and one's future possibilities often contributes to increased substance use, self-harming behaviors, and a high risk of suicide attempts.

In the face of these negative beliefs about oneself, many trans people begin to withdraw and isolate from others. This may be accompanied by betrayal, rejection, distancing, or exclusion from family of origin and religious community/family. These dynamics reinforce the pervasive message that who I am is not "OK," and certainly not loved, or valued, by the Sacred/Divine.

It is important to note that even among transgender people who have been "out" and living a rich, full, "successful" life in their authentic gender for years, the pain and self-hatred linked to embedded shame may still be reactivated by present-day experiences. It is also important to note that verbalizing this internalized shame and self-hatred after one has been "out" for some time is often a "taboo" subject. Successful trans people or leaders in the trans community are assumed to be proud of who they are and not ashamed. This community expectation can make it difficult for trans leaders to acknowledge personal experiences of shame, feelings of depression, or self-hatred. It can also make it challenging to reach out for support from peers and professionals.

My Social Location Continued

Growing up within fundamentalist Christianity, there appeared to be no way to reconcile my sexuality and gender with my Christian beliefs and my relationship with God. Everything I had been taught said that I was wrong, sinful, perverted, and suffered a mental disorder or lacked faith in God's ability to "change" me. I had two choices: deny who I was and live a lie in order to remain within my faith community or leave to live an authentic life. Despite these realities, I came out as a lesbian while at an undergraduate Bible college. Twenty years later, I came out again and transitioned to live in my affirmed male gender.

After undergrad, a new possibility emerged when I found Metropolitan Community Churches (MCC), established in 1968 as an LGBT-affirming and LGBT-identified Christian church. This community challenged me to assess and differentiate between my religious and spiritual beliefs that were damaging to me, as opposed to those supportive of my spirituality and relationship with God.

Participation within MCC through worship services, Bible studies, pastoral counseling, fellowship, and ministry opportunities consistently countered those beliefs and coping mechanisms that had been spiritually/religiously damaging within my life. These experiences and the new relationships developed with others like me simultaneously imparted and strengthened religious beliefs and practices that were healthy, renewing, and empowering in my relationships with God, myself, and others.

My Clinical Framework and Premises

Despite the many ways the fundamentalist environment in which I grew up was spiritually traumatizing, it is my belief that we cannot make assumptions about which religions/religious communities are harmful and which foster resilience, strength, and hope. There are trans-affirming "streams" within virtually every major religious tradition. We cannot let our own religious biases, assumptions, or personal narratives determine when we need to counter (or collaborate with) a client's religious beliefs and practices.

Instead, we must engage a "practice of being curious" about the role and impact of spirituality/faith/religion within the life of each transgender individual or their family. For example, many families from conservative faith communities do find ways to accept and embrace their gender diverse and transgender children. While working with a gender-fluid young adult, I found their mother reading an evangelical Christian book about demonology in our reception area. Yet, this mother and I found common ground in our shared Christian faith. Despite the conservative beliefs of her church, she was able to hold her participation in that community in tandem with unconditional love and support for her child.

My work with relational-cultural therapy (RCT) has led me to understand healthy spirituality, religious beliefs and practices, and faith communities as "growth-fostering:" they make us more alive, more authentic, more whole human beings;

they lead to increased self-acceptance and compassion for self and others; they lead to increased desire for deepened relationship to self, others, and the Divine/Sacred; they are capable of healing places of brokenness, shame, and disconnection within ourselves and our life narratives; and they lead us to greater agency and involvement in the world around us (Jordan, 2018).

Within the RCT framework, healthy, growth-fostering relationships empower us and embody the following characteristics (Miller & Stiver, 1997):

1. A sense of zest or well-being that comes from connecting with another person or other persons
2. The ability and motivation to take action in the relationship as well as other situations
3. Increased knowledge of oneself and the other person(s)
4. An increased sense of worth
5. A desire for more connections beyond this particular one

Assessment

Recognizing the negative effects of shaming religious beliefs, my stance as a family therapist is to work proactively and directly with transgender clients to assess and re-evaluate the degree to which their spirituality, religious beliefs and practices, and faith communities are healthy, particularly in the sense of being "growth-fostering."

I believe it is my responsibility to open the door to conversations about spirituality and religion and the role they have or continue to play in my client's life. This means helping transgender clients find ways to strengthen, expand, or renew those spiritual or religious beliefs and practices that enrich and empower their individual and relational lives. It also means being willing to question or challenge those spiritual or religious beliefs and practices that appear to constrain their relationships with self and others, reinforce shame and self-hatred, or inhibit increased agency and growth (Esmiol Wilson, 2018).

From an ethical perspective, this needs to be a mutual and collaborative assessment process. I need to engage my client in exploring their ideas and experiences around which spiritual/religious beliefs and practices are healing and empowering, as opposed to those that have been, or continue to be, harmful. I engage my "practice of being curious" as a way of enabling clients to assess how varying beliefs and practices have affected them. In situations where I feel it is important to challenge or counter my client's perspective, I frame my concern in terms of how it is located in my social location(s) and life history, for example, directly saying, "This is my concern and may or may not reflect your present experience."

The qualities of growth-fostering relationships offer a framework for a process of exploration and assessment with trans individuals, couples, and families. On their own or with their therapist, transgender clients can explore the overarching theme: In what ways are my spiritual/religious beliefs, practices, and community connections growth-fostering, or not, for me?

Specific questions might include:

- How can my spiritual/religious beliefs and practices contribute to a greater sense of well-being as a transgender person?
- How can I resist spiritual/religious beliefs and practices that do not strengthen my resilience?
- How can my beliefs and practices lead to increased self-authenticity and integrity?
- How can I experience a growing sense of self-worth within the context of my spiritual/religious beliefs, practices, and faith community?
- How can my spiritual/religious beliefs and practices heal feelings of shame and strengthen self-acceptance and love?
- How can my beliefs and practices contribute to greater optimism, energy, and enthusiasm for life?
- How can my spiritual/religious beliefs and practices foster greater hope for my future?
- How can my spiritual/religious beliefs and practices facilitate greater connection with myself, others, and the Divine/Sacred?
- How can my relationships within my faith community nourish, nurture, renew, and empower me?
- How can my spiritual/religious beliefs and faith community relationships empower me to take increased action within my own life to achieve my values, hopes, dreams, and sense of purpose?
- How can I experience greater self-agency within my faith community?
- How can my relationship with spirituality/religion create a desire to explore connections beyond my immediate relationships?

This assessment needs to explore the client's historical and current beliefs, practices, and relationships, both recognized and veiled internalized beliefs. Some clients explore these questions using a Likert scale; others journal about their experiences. It is important to note that the ways spiritual/religious beliefs and practices are growth-fostering often shifts and changes. What enhances our well-being at one stage may no longer do so at a later point in our life cycle.

Case Study

Charlie is a 32-year-old trans-masculine individual who grew up in a tight-knit Italian Roman Catholic working-class community. Charlie has a history of depression since adolescence and is currently experiencing significant depressive symptoms. They came to see me to resolve "confusion about my gender identity." The primary questions they wanted to explore were:

- Am I a lesbian? (This identity did not "feel right")
- Am I a "butch dyke?" (This did not "feel right" either)
- Am I a man and should I transition to live fully as a man?
- Am I a "trans-masculine" person who could live within the female body I was born into?

Charlie abandoned the church in late adolescence because it was no longer a "safe space;" they didn't feel welcome unless they pretended to be other than who they were. Despite leaving, Charlie continued to struggle with guilt and shame about their identity resulting from the internalized messages that told them who they were – as a trans-masculine individual – was not "OK," that being transgender was a sin against God that could not be forgiven. Charlie's level of distress about their gender identity and feelings of shame had reached an acute level in the months since they began participating in a trans support group at the local LGBT center.

The Effects of Internalized Religious Shame

In our first sessions, Charlie discussed how the belief that being transgender was a sin triggered painful feelings of shame about who they were and ways these feelings had impacted their life. During adolescence and young adulthood, Charlie buried these emotions with substance use and by leaving the church. While Charlie was now 3 years sober, there were numerous ways this shame had not only foreclosed clarity around gender identity but also life cycle development. For several years Charlie's religious shame and their social anxiety resulting from gender dysphoria locked them in a job they hated. They were paralyzed about looking for another job and unsure what career they wanted to pursue.

Charlie had only been in brief relationships because they believed no one would love them and they did not deserve to be in an intimate relationship. Charlie was profoundly uncomfortable with sexual intimacy and experienced acute gender dysphoria when having sex.

When Charlie was with family, they felt "unable to relax" or be authentic given their dysphoria, shame, and worry someone might ask questions about their gender identity or expression. As a result, Charlie had distanced themselves from their mother and siblings. Similar struggles played out socially, leaving Charlie with few ongoing friendships.

Spiritually Integrative Clinical Interventions

Initially Charlie's pervasive sense of shame made it difficult to talk about gender and sexuality. Consequently, we agreed the first task required "clearing away" some of this shame before we could address gender identity questions. We began by identifying religious beliefs that led to feeling shame, where these beliefs originated, and how they affected Charlie's sense of self.

During this process, I gently raised questions about specific religious beliefs:

- Is there any possibility your Catholic faith may no longer be "valid" for you? What comes up for you in reflecting on this question?
- Do you think all Roman Catholics believe being queer or transgender is a sin?
- How have these beliefs affected you and different areas of your life in the past and more recently?
- How are these beliefs helpful, growth-fostering, or empowering at this stage in your life?
- In what ways are they no longer useful or facilitate your sense of self and well-being?
- How do you imagine your life might change if you let go of certain religious beliefs that were no longer helpful to you?

As we moved through this work, we discovered Charlie also held shame-filled religious beliefs about bodies, sex, and sexuality. This exacerbated their dysphoria and ability to form, or maintain, intimate relationships. Charlie's shame-filled beliefs included the following: Sex was a sin outside of a heteronormative marriage. Queer sex was a sin. Being female-bodied and having sex with a woman was sinful. Fantasies about being sexual as a man were sinful. Though not official church teaching, Charlie had also internalized the belief that their body was sinful because of their gender identity and sexuality.

These conversations brought a range of emotions to the surface that Charlie had previously pushed aside: not only shame but also anger, hurt, and grief about the impact of these messages. Periodically, Charlie worried that "talking about all this" might mean needing to take actions they had forestalled until now.

Charlie hadn't encountered LGBT Catholics who were out and remained active within the church. I suggested several books written by LGBT Roman Catholic individuals. Reading opened up new narratives and possibilities. Not all Catholics believed being queer or having queer sex was sinful; not all LGBT Catholics felt they were beyond God's love; not all LGBT Catholics felt shame about their identity. In fact, some LGBT Catholics were proud of who they were and even able to integrate their spirituality and sexuality. Some LGBT Catholics were in same-sex relationships, or had gender transitioned, and found support within affirming parishes.

At Charlie's request, I shared information about area parishes and priests who were LGBT-affirming. Though reluctant at first, Charlie visited one of these parishes and later decided to meet one of the priests to discuss being LGBT and Catholic, including what "the church" believed about queer people. These experiences enabled Charlie to resist falling back into childhood messages that being transgender was sinful. This helped lessen their internalized shame.

How Resistance Compounds Resilience

Over time, Charlie found a new job, identified a career path, went to graduate school, and became employed in that field. Shame no longer paralyzed them or made them feel undeserving of meaningful work.

Anxious about navigating their masculine sense of self and body dysphoria, Charlie's new attempts at dating and relationships were unsatisfying. Eighteen months later Charlie met someone with whom they were able to be open about their trans-masculine identity. This support and affirmation further dissolved Charlie's shame. As a result, Charlie felt safe enough to initiate conversations about sex and sexual intimacy with this partner, including how their trans-masculine identity shaped their desire and ways they wanted to be sexually intimate.

Increased self-worth and pride led to more frequent interactions with Charlie's mother and siblings. With support and coaching, Charlie found the courage to initiate conversations about their childhood in terms of religion, gender, and sexuality. Charlie's family came to embrace their partner, including them as another couple within the family. Strengthening these relationships allowed Charlie to be increasingly involved with their niece and nephew.

Toward the end of our work, Charlie returned to mass. This enabled them to rebuild their relationship with God and the church, as well as explore new ways to integrate their spirituality, gender identity, and sexuality without shame.

Spiritually Integrative Clinical Recommendations

In addition to collaborating with transgender clients and families to evaluate the impact of their past and/or current spiritual/religious beliefs, practices, and faith communities, it is critical to empower clients to resist and recover from those that were hurtful, harming, or shaming. The following clinical interventions can facilitate healing of past spiritual/religious abuse or trauma, as well as create new rituals and practices that support their gender transition and strengthen their spiritual resilience:

- Create space(s) or rituals where transgender clients can work through grief, pain, and loss resulting from spiritual/religious experiences that contributed to gender identity suppression, disassociation, or feelings of brokenness, shame, and self-hatred.
- Create space(s) or rituals where transgender clients can express trauma-based rage toward spiritually abusive or demeaning beliefs, practices, individuals, communities, and/or the Divine/Sacred. This may require helping clients to make space within themselves for anger toward the Divine/Sacred and recognize it is "OK to be angry with God."

- Introduce transgender clients to trans-affirming spiritual or religious narratives (Beardsley & O'Brien, 2017; Martin, 2017; Mollenkott & Sheridan, 2010). For more cognitively oriented clients, doing "their own research" about alternative interpretations of sacred texts and traditions can be important (Herzer, 2016; Hornsby & Guest, 2016). Trans-affirming spiritual/religious websites often offer both information and connection that help counter negative, shaming beliefs about self and the Divine/Sacred (Muslims for Progressive Values, 2017; Trans Faith, 2017; Transtorah, 2017). For other clients, support groups and experiencing trans-affirming faith communities may be more helpful.
- Some transgender clients find ways to "reclaim" what was life-affirming and growth-fostering within their spiritual/religious upbringing.
- Encourage the use of ritual as transgender clients come out and gender transition. "Naming ceremonies" can celebrate and help transgender individuals live into their new affirmed gender and name in the world (Keshet, 2017; Pulitano, 2014). One Jewish trans man came out to his extended family during Passover by sharing the intersections of the Passover narrative of coming out of bondage and into liberation, alongside his own journey into freedom and authenticity as a trans man.
- Help transgender clients and their families explore the possibilities and risks of coming out to their faith communities and leaders. Encourage them to challenge their assumptions. Support them as they work through their fears and prepare for a range of possible responses. For example, parents who lived in a Roman Catholic immigrant community were concerned about their transgender daughter being able to take her first communion in her authentic gender. The longtime parish priest had married their parents, baptized them, married them, and baptized their children. After several discussions, the parents decided to meet with him and share their concerns. To their surprise, their priest's immediate response was, "Your child is a beloved child of God as are all children. She is welcome here as she is, and may receive her first communion as the girl God created her to be."

Concluding Thoughts

Today I am a middle-class licensed clinical social worker and family therapist working primarily with transgender children, youth, adults, and their families, an out trans social work professor at a Catholic university, and ordained clergy within Metropolitan Community Churches (MCC).

In spite of repeated religious messages that told me who I am is not "OK," I have somehow reclaimed what is healthy, healing, and affirming for my life. Today, my personal spiritual relationship, my belief that justice is love in action, and my faith in God's deeply relational and restorative presence in our world motivate and sustain both my clinical and social justice work.

Judith Butler (2004) asserts that part of the task of both feminism and queer theory *[and I would add spiritually and socially just family therapy]* is to determine "how to create a world in which those who understand their gender and their desire – their bodies – to be non-normative can live and thrive not only without the threat of violence from the outside but without the pervasive sense of their own unreality, which can lead to suicide or suicidal life" (p. 219).

As a teenager I carried a scrap of paper in my wallet with a saying on it that reflected my feelings about being in my life and my body back then. It read, "*We are the ones on whose tombs they'll inscribe, died at 15, buried at 75. Out of the depths we breathe a sigh for those who are dead, but cannot die.*" As I read these words today, I am startled by the starkness of the despair I felt about the lack of possibilities in my life. Believing oneself to be dead at 15 years, even if you will not be buried until decades later, is a "suicidal life."

Most studies indicate approximately 20–40% of homeless youth identify as LGBT, with transgender youth and youth of color disproportionately represented (Shelton, 2015; U.S. Dept. Health & Human Services, 2014). Being rejected by your family, being kicked out of your home, being bullied on a daily basis, or being homeless is a "suicidal life."

Studies within the transgender community consistently indicate 40% of trans adults have attempted suicide, compared to 1.6% of adults in the general population (James et al., 2016). One study indicated 45% of transgender youth reported suicidal thoughts and 26% had attempted suicide (Grossman & D'Augelli, 2007). The risk is higher among trans youth who have been victimized, bullied, and harassed or experienced parental/familial rejection (Grant et al., 2011).

In the context of these realities, I have embraced a professional identity as an activist, therapist, professor, and pastor – recognizing we must partner with clients in their efforts to heal from the negative effects of internalized spiritual/religious trauma and oppression and join forces in dismantling the larger religious structures that perpetuate these experiences (Hardy, 2017, p. 8). In fact, it is essential for all of us to engage in creating a world in which transgender children, youth, and adults can live and thrive without the threat of violence from the outside and without the need for suicide or a suicidal life.

References

Beardsley, C., & O'Brien, M. (Eds.). (2017). *This is my body: Hearing the theology of transgender Christians*. London: Darton, Longman, and Todd Ltd.

Butler, J. (2004). *Undoing gender*. New York: Routledge.

Esmiol Wilson, E. (2018). From assessment to activism: Utilizing a justice-informed framework to guide spiritual and religious clinical interventions. In E. Esmiol Wilson & L. A. Nice (Eds.), *Socially just religious and spiritual interventions: Ethical uses of therapeutic power, AFTA Springer Briefs*. Cham, Switzerland: Springer.

Grant, J., Mottet, L., Tanis, J., Harrison, J., Herman, J., & Keisling, M. (2011). *Injustice at every turn: A report of the National Transgender Discrimination Survey*. Washington, DC: National Center for Transgender Equality and National Gay and Lesbian Task Force.

Grossman, A. H., & D'Augelli, A. R. (2007). Transgender youth and life-threatening behaviors. *Suicide & Life-Threatening Behavior, 37*(5), 527–537.
Hardy, K. V. (2017). Naming it and claiming it: Embracing your identity as an activist (therapist, supervisor, educator). In K. V. Hardy & T. Bobes (Eds.), *Promoting cultural sensitivity in supervision: A manual for practitioners*. New York: Routledge.
Herzer. (2016). *The Bible and the transgender experience: How scripture supports gender variance*. Cleveland, OH: The Pilgrim Press.
Hornsby, T., & Guest, D. (Eds.). (2016). *Transgender, intersex, and biblical interpretation*. Atlanta, GA: SBL Press.
James, S., Herman, J., Rankin, S., Keisling, M., Mottet, L., & Anafi, M. (2016). *Executive summary of the report of the 2015 U.S. transgender survey*. Washington, DC: National Center for Transgender Equality.
Jordan, J. (2018). *Relational-cultural therapy* (2nd ed.). Washington, DC: The American Psychological Association.
Keshet. (2017). Keshet resources library. Keshet. Retrieved on December 6, 2017 from https://www.keshetonline.org/resources/
Mann, M. (2013). The nexus of stigma and social policy: Implications for pastoral care and psychotherapy with gay, lesbian, bisexual, and transgender persons and their families. *Pastoral Psychology, 62*, 199–210.
Martin, J. (2017). *Building a bridge: How the Catholic church and the LGBT community can enter into a relationship of respect, compassion, and sensitivity*. New York: HarperOne.
Miller, J. B., & Stiver, I. P. (1997). *The healing connection: How women form relationships in therapy and in life*. Boston: Beacon Press.
Mollenkott, V., & Sheridan, V. (2010). *Transgender journeys*. Eugene, OR: Resource Publications.
Mollenkott, V. (2001). *Omnigender: A trans-religious approach*. Cleveland, OH: The Pilgrim Press.
Muslims for Progressive Values. (2017). Retrieved on December 12, 2017 from http://www.mpvusa.org/lgbtqi-resources/
Pulitano, J. (2014). Transgender religious naming ceremonies. GLAAD blog. Retrieved December 6, 2017 from https://www.glaad.org/blog/transgender-religious-naming-ceremonies
Shelton, J. (2015). Transgender youth homelessness: Understanding programmatic barriers through the lens of cisgenderism. *Children and Youth Services Review, 59*, 10–18.
Singh, A., Hays, D., & Watson, L. (2011). Strength in the face of adversity: Resilience strategies of transgender individuals. *Journal of Counseling & Development, 89*(1), 20–27.
Tanis, J. (2003). *Trans-gendered: Theology, ministry, and communities of faith*. Cleveland, OH: The Pilgrim Press.
Trans Faith (2017). Retrieved on December 6, 2017 from http://www.transfaithonline.org
Transtorah. (2017). Resources. Retrieved from Transtorah website on December 6, 2017 from http://www.transtorah.org/resources.html
U.S. Dept. Health & Human Services, Administration for Children & Families, Family & Youth Services Bureau. (2014). Street outreach program: Data collection project executive summary, October 2014. Retrieved on March 21, 2016 from http://www.acf.hhs.gov/sites/default/files/fysb/fysb_sop_summary_final.pdf

Chapter 6
A Light in the Closet: Spiritually Informed Conceptual Model for Religiously Derived Mixed-Orientation Marriages

Joshua Weed and Barbara Couden Hernandez

Mixed-orientation marriage (MOM), or marriage between a person who is straight and a person who is a sexual minority, has always existed, albeit, with one individual often closeted and both living out heteronormative expectations. Recent movements in society to embrace marriage equality and to validate LGBTQIA+ populations and experiences have allowed for more open discussion regarding all relational permutations along the sexual continuum, including MOMs. Many conservative religions, including conservative Christians, feel threatened that their values and beliefs about sexual orientations other than heterosexuality are being challenged, and some even encourage efforts to change sexual orientation through conversion/reparative therapy, the harmful effects of which are well documented and have led various states to ban its practice with minors.

For sexual minorities who are religiously adherent, the tension between sexuality and faith often pits religious and cultural identity against sexual/romantic attachment identity, which can lead religious LGBTQIA+ individuals to stay in the closet and attempt to live a heteronormative life. Some religions actively encourage this, advising LGBTQIA+ individuals to marry a straight partner as one possible solution to "fix" what they label as same-sex attraction (SSA). This can be highly problematic, as such compartmentalization and rejection of sexual identity have been shown to be extremely difficult to maintain over time and can come at a high psychosocial cost (Dehlin, Galliher, Bradshaw, & Crowell, 2015). This chapter highlights the complex challenges of MOMs and illustrates a conceptual model to assist clinicians working with religiously conservative couples in MOMs.

This chapter approaches the issue of LGBTQIA+ identity and health from an affirming stance that aligns with the APA's statement regarding sexual orientation. This statement affirms the legitimacy of variations of sexual orientation and states, among other

J. Weed (✉)
Private Marriage and Family Therapy Practice in Kent, Kent, WA, USA

B. C. Hernandez
Loma Linda University School of Medicine, Loma Linda, CA, USA

E. Esmiol Wilson, L. Nice (eds.), *Socially Just Religious and Spiritual Interventions*, AFTA SpringerBriefs in Family Therapy, https://doi.org/10.1007/978-3-030-01986-0_6

important items, that "…the prejudice and discrimination that people who identify as lesbian, gay or bisexual regularly experience have been shown to have negative psychological effects" (American Psychological Association, 2008). That said, this chapter is not intended to solve the dilemma of whether or not a clinician can be an ethical practitioner and hold the belief that same-sex relationships are sinful. Couples in MOMs can be strongly convicted in multiple ways over the course of their relationship, as demonstrated by the case presentation. Our hope is that this chapter invites a continued dialogue about how therapists can work with clients at whichever stage they present to help them find greater relational connection and personal congruence.

Social Location and Context of Authors

I (JW) am a 38-year-old, cisgender, gay, white male therapist and writer who is a member of the LDS church. I have worked extensively with MOMs clinically and was in a MOM myself. I (BH) am a 60-year-old cisgender, heterosexual, white therapist educator who is a member of a Seventh-day Adventist congregation. I have worked clinically with MOM couples and also have been deeply affected by the dissolution of a relative's MOM. Both authors' clinical and personal experience have more often involved couples with gay men married to heterosexual women in a religious context. We therefore have narrowed the focus of this chapter to religious gay men in MOMs. We acknowledge that MOM can include sexual orientations all along the LGBTQIA+ continuum and can involve either religious or nonreligious couples. However, configurations beyond those involving religious gay men married to women fall outside the scope of this chapter. Although we refer most specifically to gay men in our cited research and case study, we employ the acronym LGBTQIA+ where possible to highlight the variability of potential sexual orientation expression in MOM.

Understanding Mixed-Orientation Marriages

MOMs Among Religious Conservatives

LGBTQIA+ individuals in conservative religious contexts are taught that all forms of sexual expression other than heterosexuality repel God. Over a quarter of religious LGBTQIA+ youth are disowned because their parents cannot reconcile their religious perspectives with their children's sexuality, significantly affecting their spirituality (Vanderwaal, Sedlacek, & Lane, 2017). Parental rejection leads to higher rates of substance abuse, high-risk sexual behavior, depression, and suicide (Eisenberg & Resnick, 2006; Ryan, Huebner, Diaz, & Sanchez, 2009) and a sense of spiritual loss (Vanderwaal et al., 2017). It should not be surprising that conservative religious young adults might marry in the hopes of being able to avoid judgment, rejection, and marginalization.

Approximately two million MOMs existed as of 2001 (Buxton, 2001). Gay men who were once married to a woman are more likely to have come from a fundamentalist religious background (Higgins, 2004). For example, Orthodox Jewish gay men are often encouraged by their rabbi to marry in order to hide their same-sex attraction (Kissil & Itzhaky, 2014). These marriages are focused on adherence to religious requirements for desirable family function and community standing. Study participants reported feeling respect and tenderness in their marriages, but none reported erotic feelings toward their wives. Most did not tell their wives of their same-sex attraction, and those who did reported that neither raised the issue again after the initial disclosure.

The Church of Jesus Christ of Latter-day Saints (LDS) or Mormon Church includes LGBTQIA+ individuals in its membership who forego same-sex relationships and experiences and who are willing to conceptualize their draw toward members of the same sex as merely "attractions" and not part of a broader sexual/romantic attachment identity. Individuals in same-sex relationships are not allowed to become church members, and members of the LDS church who choose to marry partners of the same sex are excommunicated, while children raised by same-sex parents are required to renounce their parents' marriage if they wish to join the church (Goodstein, 2015). Other religious groups that forbid same-sex marriages include Southern Baptists, Muslims, Jehovah's Witnesses, Seventh-day Adventists, Eastern Orthodox, the American Reformed Church, Missouri Synod Lutheran, Assembly of God, Apostolic and Pentecostal groups, and many Evangelical nondenominational congregations. Those in MOM who come out to their congregation often face insensitivity, marginalization, or judgment (Hernandez & Wilson, 2007).

Challenges of Sexual Reorientation and Maintaining MOMs

When options are limited, many LGBTQIA+ adolescents learn to hide their sexual orientation early on and may engage in seemingly heterosexual relationships. In one study, researchers found that 70% of sexual minority students abstained from any same-sex behavior (Yarhouse, Stratton, Dean, & Brooke, 2009). In another study, researchers identified two motivations for gay men to marry straight women: to further their denial of same-sex attraction or to fulfill the heterosexual ideal of marriage (Ortiz and Scott, 1994). Because of the complex religious and sexual identity stressors that occur during mixed-orientation dating and marriage, many individuals seek therapy. When this therapy includes efforts to change one's sexual orientation, there are clear and often severe consequences. Not only do these efforts increase risks for the client, but they are largely ineffective in the overall, long-term goal of sexual reorientation (Jones & Yarhouse, 2007; Bradshaw, Dehlin, Crowell, & Galliher, 2015).

Approximately a third of couples in MOMs divorce within the 1st year after coming out, a third separate after 2 years, and a third decide to remain married (Buxton, 2006). At least half of those who do remain together are divorced within 3 years with relationship quality described as somewhat distressed (Kays, Yarhouse, & Ripley, 2014). The divorce rate of MOMs has been reported as high as nearly 70% (Dehlin, Galliher, Bradshaw, & Crowell, 2014). Bisexual women may be able to sustain MOM longer than lesbians due to the expectation of attraction to both men and women as part of their marriage (Buxton, 2004). The straight partner in a MOM often experiences unique challenges, such as understanding their own sexuality, responding with integrity, making sense of this given their belief system (Buxton, 2006), and maintaining a sense of sexual desirability (Hernandez & Wilson, 2007). Shared challenges between partners may include discussing this with children or other family members and struggling through religious and spiritual implications.

Challenges Coming Out in MOMs

When the LGBTQIA+ partner in a religiously influenced MOM comes out, both partners may wonder how they could have misread signs from God that they should marry, leaving them feeling spiritually disoriented (Hernandez & Wilson, 2007). The LGBTQIA+ spouse may feel betrayed by God for failing to change their sexual orientation or prevent the pain that their coming out has brought to a partner they may genuinely love. Straight spouses may feel that their marriage has been a "sham" even while acknowledging the positive aspects of their partnership. Well-intentioned loved ones from a variety of belief systems may suggest that the couple should never have gotten married in the first place or that they should have worked harder to make their MOM work.

Therapy with MOM Couples

Conservative religious MOM couples often privilege the straight partner's religiously acceptable heteronormative perspectives and minimize the validity of the LGBTQIA+ partner's experience. Many MOM couples who present for therapy are anxious, emotionally disorganized, and in pain. Therapists who rush to support divorce rather than help MOM couples deconstruct and renegotiate meanings around marriage, femininity, masculinity, and sex, or consider how these may be similar or different in a typical heterosexual marriage over time may miss important therapeutic connections (Wolkomir, 2009). Highlighting strengths and supportive relationships to nurture hope can help, as can acknowledging frightening emotional responses to a very real dilemma. The perception and meaning of events often play a significant role in the degree of crisis, as do the coping skills and available support systems (Bigner, 2006).

MOM couples often couch their situation in religious terms and miss other important elements at play. Doherty's work (2009) suggests that such clients benefit from considering at least two other perspectives from which to process their concerns: the moral perspective that includes values of honesty, responsibility, devotion, etc. and the clinical perspective that includes mental health benefits of various behaviors, family patterns, symptoms, stages of adjustment, and well-being. Spiritually sensitive interventions are needed to help couples systematically examine their religious beliefs as well as to deconstruct heteropatriarchy that frames their approach to MOM (Esmiol Wilson, 2018). Couples may reactively discard all religious beliefs rather than carefully consider how they can incorporate cherished or important elements of their faith into their decision-making. Critical reflection on these often unquestioned, core beliefs is necessary to forge a new sense of self in relation to others and create a more authentic healing and supportive outlook informed by spiritual integrity.

Other challenging issues to explore include the coming out and adjustment process such as concern for how children will respond, the straight spouse's concern for their partner's well-being at the expense of their own well-being, the experience of ambiguous loss, and the spiritual questioning and growth that can occur (Hernandez & Wilson, 2007).

Conceptual Framework and Case Study

The lifespan of most religious-based MOMs has been divided into three different phases. These are not necessarily linear, and providers are cautioned against assuming that all MOM couples will experience things in this way or that progression through the stages linearly equates religious maturity. This paradigm is limited in that it cannot account for the complex realities of the spectra it attempts to circumscribe. It does not effectively account for the massive variations possible in two individuals' respective locations on the Kinsey scale, for example—generalizing to "straight partner and LBGTQIA+ partner." Nor does this model fully account for the wide range of variables involved in religious and spiritual journeys such as the ways that personal characteristics intersect with one's experience of religion and spirituality, experience with oppression, abuse, or privilege. What it does provide is a generalized conceptual framework for religious-based MOMs that will help anchor a clinician's approach when working with clients of this population.

The process outlined is heavily informed by my (JW) extensive clinical work with MOM clients over the last 5 years, after I came out as part of a MOM couple in a blog that went viral. The case example I use to demonstrate this process will diverge from the norm insofar as, instead of referring to a client with whom I have worked, I will refer to my own experience in a MOM. Below I illustrate this process by sharing a brief description of each stage in the conceptual model, and then a corresponding case study from my own relationship with my ex-wife, Lolly, who likes me is a practicing MFT and has given me permission to share our story.

Phase I: Religious Adherence and Conformity

In this phase, strict religious adherence and conformity to religious culture guide decision-making. Religious adherence and cultural conformity are also the lens used for interpretation of alternative sexual orientation to the degree that it is recognized by either partner. Many couples come from religions that discourage appropriate language around sexual minority status (e.g., gay, lesbian, bi, LGBTQIA+, etc.) instead of favoring reductive terms like same-sex attracted (SSA) or same-gender attracted (SGA). This enables adherents to speak of the behavioral phenomena they are seeing without it being connected to identity, personality, romance, or a true sense of self. If there is sexual acting-out on the part of the LGBTQIA+ partner, it is often done in secret (DeVore & Blumenfeld, 2014), and LGBTQIA+ sexual experiences are thought of as sinful choices rather than indicators of a congruent sexual orientation. The broader LGBTQIA+ community is often seen by the couple—as per the lens of religious narrative—as a threat to family, God, and correct living.

Phase I of Our Story Lolly and I married in 2002. As Mormons, we had grown up on the same street in Utah, and our fathers had been good friends as they served in church lay leadership capacities together. I had outed myself to Lolly at the age of 16, having also outed myself to my parents at the age of 13 (this is unusual for most MOMs—many times the LGBTQIA+ partner does not come out until during the course of the marriage). While my parents and Lolly supported me and I could clearly feel their love and acceptance, our shared Mormon perspective informed all of the discussions we had about this issue. As I spoke to church leaders as well as LDS therapists (many of whom had training in techniques of conversion therapy during this time period), there was a consensus around how to approach my "same-sex attraction" (SSA) that was informed by the doctrines of the Mormon faith. As a collective, this group viewed my "SSA" as a problem that could be "corrected" with enough prayer, fasting, faith, and counseling.

Through this process of attempted conversion from gay to straight, Lolly was my ally and advocate. By the time we were both in college at Brigham Young University, Idaho, my therapist at the school encouraged me to start dating girls. I did so. I had never been with a man, and thus I had no basis of comparison for these dating experiences. They were not exciting in the ways I could tell pursuing men would have been, but they were also not entirely repulsive experiences. I got a girlfriend, and when we kissed, I even had a small stirring of sexual response. As Lolly saw me increasingly taking on what I thought were "straight" ways of being in the world, she began to view me as a potential romantic partner. Eventually we dated and married, hoping that my deep, platonic love for her might someday grow into sexual attraction.

Lolly and I worked hard at our marriage—going on frequent dates, engaging in emotional vulnerability, and ensuring that we were sexually intimate often. Only in retrospect can I look back and realize that beneath all of the denial I'd scaffolded as the infrastructure sustaining this sex life that defied my actual sexual orientation was a profound sense, each time, of incongruence, sadness, and loss—an unsettling discomfort that I was loathe to acknowledge, preferring to hope that as the years passed, it would go away. As a straight person, whose sexual orientation had been affirmed throughout her life, Lolly *did* notice that something was missing from time to time, but anytime she vocalized her worries, I had no framework to understand what she was saying. I really did believe this was as good as it would get, or at very least, that it was a sufficient replacement for authentic sexual connection with a man.

Phase II: Continued Religious Adherence with Growing Spiritual Nuance

In this phase, religious adherence and cultural conformity are still strong; however, couples often experience an increase of awareness around the LGBTQIA+ partner's orientation and a profound sense of loss over an understanding of the permanence of this. Sexual orientation may be explained as a burden to bear and is often compared to things like alcoholism or overeating: a "desire of the flesh." Some LGBTQIA+ partners may maintain hope for orientational change in the afterlife. This growing acceptance of the static nature of the LGBTQIA+ client's orientation (still often referred to as SSA during this stage) leads to increased feelings of distress as they realize that their marriage to someone of a different sexual orientation will mean never experiencing full sexual or romantic expression. Other challenging issues may include deeply held beliefs about the sanctity of marriage and prohibitions on divorce, as well as concern over the continued well-being of one's partner through these stressful experiences. Emerging spiritual dilemmas may include new questions on how God might permit the suffering experienced by many earnestly religious LGBTQIA+ people without allowing for the "healing" for which they have fervently prayed. These shifts generally serve to increase the self-acceptance of the LGBTQIA+ spouse. This would normally positively impact mental health symptoms, except that it also increases the distress of the straight spouse, reinforcing the bind and entrapment that both parties begin to experience more explicitly.

Phase II of Our Story At 10 years of marriage (in 2012), Lolly and I chose to come out to our local religious and professional communities about the unique nature of our marriage through a blog post. To our great shock, this went viral, and we received an onslaught of media attention. While we were always careful to explain that our choice was our own, and not a template to follow, our story was frequently used by religious people to pressure their LGBTQIA+ loved ones to marry against their orientation. This was deeply distressing to us. Even through all of this, renegotiation of my own MOM with Lolly was incomprehensible to me. We had felt very clearly that God had wanted us to marry, and our faith in God and willingness to do what he asked of us was a mutually shared moral imperative that was still largely connected to religious adherence for us.

After the blog post, my client load-shifted and I worked heavily with MOM clients. In so doing, I began to see a pattern of couples caught a double bind. As the LGBTQIA+ partner denied their sexual orientation, they suffered symptoms of depression, anxiety, unwanted sexual behaviors, repeat infidelity, sideways manifestations of inappropriate sexual expression with same-sex partners (including minors), and suicidality. Conversely, as LGB clients accepted this part of themselves by sharing more of their true feelings/thoughts/attractions with their spouse, finding outside support and community around "this struggle," coming out publicly, etc., the heterosexual spouse's mental health deteriorated and the marriages suffered. Neither of these situations seemed fair to the parties involved, who were often deeply religious individuals whose spiritual lives were rich and real, and whose relationships together had been entered into in good faith on both sides, and had often been experienced as generous, loving, genuine, and authentic to the degree their respective romantic/sexual attachment orientations had allowed.

Phase III: Full Spiritual Nuance with Modified Religious Adherence

In this phase, the strain of the growing distress felt by both partners as the LGBTQIA+ partner accepts their sexual orientation as a critical part of identity begins to push the marriage to a breaking point. Denial is low, and awareness of unmet sexual/romantic attachment needs becomes excruciating and incessant for both parties. Couples who attempt to continue in this state over time often experience symptoms of high distress, such as suicidal ideation or reckless infidelity that goes against long-held religious and spiritual values. Faced with potential outcomes such as this, some couples may opt for divorce. Other couples may renegotiate marital terms to allow for both partners to develop romantic relationships outside of their own. These changes can cause significant shifts in couples' experiences of religion and spirituality. Some may view their religious foundation as spiritually abusive and may struggle with feelings of anger and sadness. Others may feel a profound sense of loss at a religious community that "loves the sinner but hates the sin." Still others may choose to stay in their religious community while living in ways not supported by religious doctrine.

Phase III of Our Story Last fall, I watched a dear friend of mine, a lesbian, who had chosen to exit her own long-standing MOM, fall in love with a woman for the first time. Through a series of epiphanies that were as devastating to our shared hopes and dreams as they were freeing and enlightening, Lolly and I realized that even though I had known I was gay since puberty, there were still levels of denial we were engaging in that kept both of us from living congruently. In essence, there were pockets of internal self-hatred and disapproval around my gayness that had remained unexamined, which as Lolly and I talked, came to light. When I realized this and saw the level of my dormant internalized homophobia, I broke down. I allowed myself to see the levels to which my adherence to this part of Mormonism and even my participation in our marriage were preventing me from full actualization and acceptance of this critical part of my true identity.

I was stunned most of all when, during this conversation, I saw a text message I'd sent to my straight best friend the week before that said, "I have thought of putting a gun in my mouth more times than I can count." Reading those words aloud felt like reading words written by another person—but they weren't; they were *my* words. The seriousness weighed down on me fully for the first time. I cried for hours with Lolly as we held each other until we fell asleep. I was despondent for many days, unable to get out of bed, as the implications of this removal of denial concussively racked my awareness, and I realized what it meant. Lolly and I then spent significant time processing the effects of our MOM, which included my recurrent, attachment-based suicidal ideation and Lolly's growing depression around the experience of deep romantic and sexual rejection by me.

As we made the decision to divorce lying together in our living room, weeping in each other's arms, we grieved the loss of our family structure and the implications of this for our four daughters. We wept with pain, but also with relief, as we realized that this meant that we could both find partners to love and be loved by in return and that we no longer had to ache as we watched the couples all around us enjoy the fruits of orientational compatibility. Seeing this in those around us had become especially painful as we'd attempted to navigate the complexities that had emerged in recent years, like the fact that since my mom had passed away the year before I had been unable to engage in sex, and didn't know when, or if, I'd ever be able to again.

For us, the solution that felt right was to divorce. However, this shift required modification of our religious adherence, especially for me. I am now viewed as a "sinner" by our faith community, and because Lolly supports me, she might be viewed as complicit in this. Furthermore, I know that if I ever marry again, I will be excommunicated from the Mormon faith, and my children may not be allowed to be baptized until they turned 18 and renounce my marriage. In spite of this, for both of us, there is a resounding sense of spiritual approbation to the measures we were taking. It feels very clear that this is God's will and plan for us, and there is even a sense that it was the plan all along. Realizing that living in my sexual identity was always God's intention for me helps me see the ways that I, as a gay man, was never actually "invited to the table" of Mormonism to begin with. Because of this, I find that the LDS church's institutional assessment of me as a gay man matters less to me. Thus, while Mormonism was my vehicle to gain spirituality and a connection with God, I no longer see it as my liaison between God and myself, nor do I feel it is equipped to effectively arbitrate that relationship. I still attend, I still worship, and I still connect to this part of my personal and family identity, spanning many generations. But I no longer feel beholden to this institutional entity that has never actually accepted me for who I am in the way I can now clearly feel that God himself does.

Conclusion

MOM is promoted by some as an alternative lifestyle arrangement that should be given validity the same as any other. While Lolly and I were in Phase I and part of Phase 2, we strongly advocated for this stance as a legitimate, spiritually congruent option. However, what a person defines as legitimate and spiritually just can change over time. Knowing what we know personally and clinically about MOMs, it is now our shared belief that the increase of suicidality and depression is too common, the success rates are too low, and the requirements of potentially toxic levels of incongruence, denial, and internalized homophobia are too great to be proffered as a generalizable option to LGB individuals. This is especially true when we take into account that, just as in my case, it is often presented as a viable option by straight persons of influence such as religious leaders, parents, or religiously adherent conversion therapists. These vulnerable youth and young adults are attempting normal development as they try to understand their nonheterosexual sexual/romantic attachment orientation within a religious context. Viewed in this light, the offering up MOM as one of the "solutions" to sexual minority status alongside celibacy as the only other religiously congruent "solution" by those in power is clearly problematic.

Therapists working with MOM couples should remember that the model outlined in this chapter may not fit for every couple and that partners may not move through the phases linearly or together or at all. We recommend that all therapists working with MOM couples do extensive self-of-the-therapist work to look deeply at their own personal responses to these issues; as for many of us, they reflect our deepest and strongest values. Therapists should also educate themselves on the religious and spiritual background unique to each couple and recognize that for strong cultural religions (like Mormonism), the loss endemic to coming out may be especially extensive. It is also important to remember that therapists may thoughtfully and respectfully help clients untangle core identity and attachment needs from harmful religious doctrine, as well as from ecclesiastical leaders or therapists who may have had undue influence in the creation of a MOM. We recognize that this work is not neutral and reaffirm the need for therapists to move forward with continued self-reflection and checking in with self and with clients. In this way, in contrast to prior experiences where people with power have exerted undue influence, clinicians can provide assistance to these vulnerable clients and tenderly guide and assist in a manner that is truly spiritually just.

References

American Psychological Association. (2008). *Answers to your questions: For a better understanding of sexual orientation and homosexuality*. Washington, DC: American Psychological Association. Retrieved from www.apa.org/topics/lgbt/orientation.pdf

Bigner, J. J. (2006). Disclosing gay or lesbian orientation within marriage: A systems perspective. In C. A. Everett & R. E. Lee (Eds.), *When marriage fail: Systemic family therapy interventions and issues: A tribute to William C. Nichols* (pp. 85–100). New York: Haworth Press.

Bradshaw, K., Dehlin, J. P., Crowell, K. A., & Galliher, R. V. (2015). Sexual orientation change efforts through psychotherapy for LGBQ individuals affiliated with The Church of Jesus Christ of Latter-day Saints. *Journal of Sex & Marital Therapy, 41*(4), 391–412.

Buxton, A. P. (2001). Writing our own script: How bisexual men and their heterosexual wives maintain their marriages after disclosure. *Journal of Bisexuality, 1*(2–3), 155–189.

Buxton, A. (2004). Works in progress: How mixed-orientation couples maintain their marriages after the wives come out. *Journal of Bisexuality, 4*(1–2), 57–82.

Buxton, A. (2006). When a spouse comes out: Impact on the heterosexual partner. *Sexual Addiction & Compulsivity, 13*(2/3), 317–332.

Dehlin, J. P., Galliher, R. V., Bradshaw, W. S., & Crowell, K. A. (2014). Psychosocial correlates of religious approaches to same-sex attraction: A Mormon perspective. *Journal of Gay & Lesbian Mental Health, 18*(3), 284–311.

Dehlin, J. P., Galliher, R. V., Bradshaw, W. S., & Crowell, K. A. (2015). Navigating sexual and religious identity conflict: A Mormon perspective. *Identity, 15*(1), 1–22.

DeVore, E., & Blumenfeld, W. (2014). The family, conservative Christianity, and resilience of lesbian and gay youth: A qualitative study. In A. Dessel & R. Bolen (Eds.), *Conservative Christian beliefs and sexual orientation in social work*. Alexandria, VA: Council on Social Work Education Press.

Doherty, W. J. (2009). Morality and spirituality in therapy. In F. Walsh (Ed.), *Spiritual resources in family therapy* (2nd ed., pp. 215–228). New York: Guilford Press.

Eisenberg, M., & Resnick, M. (2006). Suicidality among gay, lesbian, and bisexual youth: The role of protective factors. *Journal of Adolescent Health, 39*, 662–668.

Esmiol Wilson, E. (2018). From assessment to activism: Utilizing a justice-informed framework to guide spiritual and religious clinical interventions. In E. Esmiol Wilson & L. A. Nice (Eds.), *Socially just religious and spiritual interventions: Ethical uses of therapeutic power, AFTA Springer Briefs*. Cham, Switzerland: Springer.

Goodstein, L. (2015). Mormons sharpen stand against same sex marriage. *New York Times*.

Hernandez, B. C., & Wilson, C. M. (2007). Another kind of ambiguous loss: Seventh-day Adventist women in mixed-orientation marriages. *Family Relations, 56*, 184–195.

Higgins, D. J. (2004). Differences between previously married and never married 'gay' men: Family background, childhood experiences, and current attitudes. *Journal of Homosexuality, 48*, 19–41.

Jones, S. L., & Yarhouse, M. A. (2007). *Ex-gays?* Downers Grove, IL: IVP.

Kays, J. L., Yarhouse, M. A., & Ripley, J. S. (2014). Relationship factors and quality among mixed-orientation couples. *Journal of Sex & Marital Therapy, 40*(6), 512–528.

Kissil, K., & Itzhaky, H. (2014). Experiences of the marital relationship among orthodox Jewish gay men in mixed-orientation marriages. *Journal of GLBT Family Studies*. https://doi.org/10.1080/1550428X.2014.900659

Ortiz, E. T., & Scott, P. R. (1994). Gay husbands and fathers: Reasons for marriage among homosexual men. *Journal of Gay and Lesbian Social Services, 1*, 59–71.

Ryan, C., Huebner, D., Diaz, R., & Sanchez, J. (2009). Family rejection as a predictor of negative health outcomes in White and Latino lesbian, gay and bisexual young adults. *Pediatrics, 123*(1), 346–352.

Vanderwaal, C. J., Sedlacek, D., & Lane, L. (2017). The impact of family rejection or acceptance among LGBT+ millennials in the Seventh-day Adventist church. *Social Work & Christianity, 44*(1&2), 72–95.

Wolkomir, M. (2009). The story of romantic love, sexuality, and gender in mixed-orientation marriages. *Gender & Society, 23*(4), 494–519.

Yarhouse, M. A., Stratton, S. P., Dean, J. B., & Brooke, H. L. (2009). Listening to sexual minorities on Christian College campuses. *Journal of Psychology and Theology, 37*(2), 96–113.

Chapter 7
Reconnecting After an Affair: Relationship Justice, Spirituality, and Infidelity Treatment

Kirstee Williams

Roughly half of couples seeking therapy come to treatment for an affair (Weeks, Gambescia, & Jenkins, 2003). Fortunately, the literature available on how to work with affairs is extensive (e.g., Snyder, Baucom, & Gordon, 2007; Snyder & Doss, 2005; Weeks et al., 2003). Yet, the intersectionality between spirituality, infidelity, and couple recovery is less known. The literature has only recently begun to address issues of relational justice as it relates to gender and power in affair recovery (Williams, 2011; Williams, Galick, Knudson-Martin, & Huenergardt, 2012; Williams & Knudson-Martin, 2012). There are models that focus on forgiveness (e.g., Fife, Weeks, & Stellberg-Filbert, 2011), but specifically spirituality influences treatment, and recovery is seldom addressed.

In this chapter I present a framework for addressing issues of gender, power, spirituality, and affairs in couples' treatment and recovery. I developed an interest in the integration of spirituality and relational justice as I teach and practice in the South where a traditional Christian model often prioritizes both my students' and clients' life choices and relationship structures. I am the director and assistant professor of the first COAMFTE-accredited program in my state and work for a university that is faith based. I am also the only female core faculty member in our marriage and family therapy program. I identify as a Christian, yet I am highly sensitive and attuned toward social justice concerns such as gender issues, power inequalities, and cultural diversity. I am heterosexual, and like the majority of the professors at my institution, I am White.

My private practice consists mainly of middle class, white, and heterosexual couples, almost all of whom come to therapy seeking treatment for a variety of affair-related issues. In a conservative, faith-based community such as ours, the majority of my clients strive to follow a traditional Christian relationship structure

K. Williams (✉)
Department of Behavioral and Social Sciences, Lee University, Cleveland, TN, USA
e-mail: kirsteewilliams@leeuniversity.edu

E. Esmiol Wilson, L. Nice (eds.), *Socially Just Religious and Spiritual Interventions*, AFTA SpringerBriefs in Family Therapy, https://doi.org/10.1007/978-3-030-01986-0_7

with husband as the head of the home and wife as support. Most of my couples are perplexed to find that this type of faith-based relationship structure does not protect them from affairs, and thus integrating spirituality, gender, and power becomes a central theme of much of my work.

Integration of Social Justice and Infidelity Treatment

Infidelity cannot be understood without exploring the societal processes that influence both the etiology of affairs and recovery from them (i.e., permissive sexual values, being male, opportunity, gender inequality, and cultural norms) (Atkins, Baucom, & Jacobson, 2001; Glass, 2003; Treas & Giesen, 2000; Williams, 2011). When these contextual factors are not conceptualized, responsibility tends to be placed equally on both partners for setting the stage for an affair (e.g., Brown, 2005; Moultrup, 2005; Olmstead, Blick, & Mills, 2009). Feminist scholars have long critiqued family systems for ignoring sociocultural processes that unintentionally assume equality in couple structures when they are not inherently equal (e.g., Goldner, 1985; Hare-Mustin, 1978). Yet, it is difficult for couples and clinicians to recognize how power inequalities structure their interaction (Knudson-Martin & Mahoney, 2009) as patriarchal ideals are often embedded within a traditional gendered and Christian world view.

The connections between infidelity and power have also been documented in research (e.g., Lammers, Stoker, Jordan, Pollmann, & Stapel, 2011). Results indicate that elevated power is positively associated with affairs as it increases risk-taking behaviors, confidence in one's ability to attract a potential partner, and opportunity for an affair (Lammers et al., 2011). In fact, the relationship between power and infidelity is so strong that gender differences in who has affairs become void in light of this positive correlation (Lammers et al., 2011). For example, as women move up the corporate ladder, the likelihood that they would be unfaithful matches that of men. Therefore, recognizing the relationship between power, inequality, and infidelity is an essential element of integrating social justice in affair recovery.

Integration of Social Justice and Spirituality in Infidelity Treatment

Exploring the connections between social justice and spirituality in infidelity recovery is virtually nonexistent. While clinicians recognize the importance of the role that spirituality plays in couple's lives, few of us know how to either counter harmful spiritual beliefs or utilize spirituality as an asset in affair recovery. This has been a journey for me, as I continue to work with predominately Christian couples and as my own Christian world view has shifted over time. My shift involved prioritizing spirituality in affair work by recognizing how dominate Christian discourses organize one's relational stance which ultimately impacts affair recovery. This shift helped me realize that I have not always seen the necessity of integrating spirituality into my clinical work. Even with Christian clients, exploring intersections of faith and religion with the presenting problem was not something I specifically focused on in session. My approach has changed, as I have seen how organizing spiritual discourses are especially relevant as they relate to affairs.

Working Knowledge of the Bible

A central element of my current work with Christian clients is to ensure that I have a working knowledge of the Bible. What I mean by this is the same ways in which we study infidelity, understand trauma, and work to know the processes by which we can best support couple recovery; it is helpful to have an active knowledge of the main biblical themes, discourses, and narratives to which our clients subscribe. Therapists can hold a different faith or not subscribe to any faith and still effectively work with faith-based clients. What is essential however is exploring a client's faith and religious world view. In Chap. 1 (Esmiol Wilson, 2018), the author outlines several helpful questions for exploring client's religious realities, such as: (1) What are some important spiritual/religious beliefs you hold? (2) How do your beliefs impact your relationships? (3) How do you image the divine or sacred sees you and feels about you? (4) Describe any beliefs you hold that feel difficult or conflicting (p. 7).

Separating Harmful and Healing Christian Influences

I have found for most of my clients their Christianity plays a dual role contributing to subtle inequalities and at the same time a vital resource for healing. Those traditional religious discourses that support inequality must be unpacked and understood within the context of the affair. But other religious discourses that support unity and connectedness through Christlike love, humility, and self-sacrifice are essential narratives to draw upon that support mutuality. I have found most often my couples are seeking to be Christlike in their marriages but become confused or disillusioned along the way simply because they do not understand how their faith is organizing their daily interactions. Thus, unpacking often rigid, faith-based power disparities is central to treatment and necessary in order for healing Christian values to simultaneously emerge.

A Spiritually Informed Framework

I have found it helpful to conceptualize my work with affairs as a three-phase process: (1) creating an equitable foundation for healing, (2) placing infidelity in a social context, and (3) practicing mutuality (Williams, 2011; Williams et al., 2012). While this model originally did not directly address faith integration, this chapter outlines how spirituality fits within this framework.

Most of my Christian clients who are in affairs violate their own moral and ethical standards and struggle to understand why and how they got there. Therefore, we begin by unpacking specific beliefs that are linked to inequality, such as "men is the head of the home or women are supposed to serve their husbands." This is done in first phase of my affair model as we work through crisis and begin creating the equitable foundation for healing. In the second phase I make the connection between power and affairs more explicit for the couple by highlighting how their beliefs organize their relationship structure and ultimately the infidelity. The aim of this is twofold: first to separate the person from their affair as their guilt and shame are often overwhelming and second to help the couple understand how aspects of their traditionally held Christian values may be linked to subtle inequalities in their partnership that contributed, almost always subconsciously, to the affair. Phase III involves helping the couple integrate their learning as they work to reorganize their relational structure in practice. For example, a husband with limited vulnerability practices vulnerability in session, ultimately leading to new and ongoing relationship patterns.

Case Example: Challenges of Integrating Social Justice into Religious Theology

Bonnie and Arthur sit across from me in my office. Bonnie's head is down, her gray hair rumpled from running her hands through it. "I just don't know what to do anymore" she sobs, "I don't know how to reconcile this in my mind and I feel completely and utterly alone." Arthur, looking just as desperate as Bonnie, tries to offer some halfhearted words of assurance, but these quickly trail off in silence as his shame overwhelms him. Bonnie continues without looking up, "You brought her to my home! I welcomed her into our home! How could you?" Bonnie is so angry she refuses to look at Arthur. "I have raised your children, cooked your meals, washed your clothes, and this, after 50 years of marriage is how you repay me?!"

Bonnie and Arthur are in their early 70s. They are White Southerners and devout Christians, and for 49 of their 50 years of marriage Arthur has been faithful. After retiring Arthur spent some time "finding himself" which led to a temporary job as a sales manager for a large company. Here he met a young, mid-20s something youth, who paid him special attention as the incoming manager. His first instinct was to invite this young woman to church, praising himself for "saving" this wayward youth. Yet, as time continued and the young woman began to return the advances, things heated up quickly for Arthur, and soon he found himself contemplating leaving his wife of 50 years for a month-long fling that ended when the temp worker left the job to go to travel. Here is where he confessed his sin to Bonnie and before God.

As I listened to the narrative I knew how critical it was to help Bonnie and Arthur integrate their Christian faith with both an understanding of the affair and their healing process. Bonnie and Arthur, like most of my Christian couples, experienced their faith as the organizing principle by which they lived their lives. While Arthur deeply valued the biblical stance of loving his wife as Christ loved the church (Ephesians 5:25), he also deeply valued his role as head of the home. This power position ultimately limited his accountability and vulnerability with Bonnie. Thus, after the process of stabilization which involved moving past the initial crisis of discovery, it was important to help both partners begin to understand the intersection of their faith and Arthur's affair.

Phase I: Creating an Equitable Foundation for Relational and Spiritual Healing

The goal in this first stage of work is to set the stage for mutual healing (Williams, 2011; Williams et al., 2012). Typically following the discoveries surrounding an affair, crisis management and stabilization are at the forefront of the work. Yet, as couples stabilize, continued stabilization requires creating that equitable foundation for healing. I think of this as making sure I am not showing preference for one person over the other which usually incorporates giving voice to the partner who is or has been more traditionally silenced.

For Bonnie and Arthur this was especially important as Bonnie was torn between expressing her anger and dismissing her anger in order to protect Arthur's shame. I knew that first I had to create a context of awareness of equality yet facilitate an environment that supported both people to feel heard and understood (Williams, 2011). For this couple, creating a context of awareness meant helping them both understand the subtle inequalities that existed as they adhered to the commonly held belief that men should have the final say and are entitled to an ongoing level of privacy in their personal and business endeavors. Supporting both Author and Bonnie in feeling heard meant helping them recognize areas of feeling silenced. For Bonnie, this was easy to see as she felt the effects of her subservient life yet lacked the language to describe her experience. For Arthur, it meant identifying those aspects in his life where he felt isolated and alone due to his inability to access his vulnerability easily and overburdened with the decisions regarding the financial stability of the household.

Arthur had to further allow room for guilt and shame to enter into the conversation. Both he and Bonnie actively fought to pull him away from feeling any sense of shame as his Christian values as head of the home limited his vulnerability, and his "maleness" intersected to privilege this protection.

Therapist: Arthur, I recognize that these feelings of guilt are overwhelming but I am so glad you are here and talking about the shame. I realize it's not easy. I am going to ask you a difficult question so you can take a minute to prepare: I want to know how is it for you to have violated your spiritual and ethical code in this way?

Arthur: It's not something I like to think about. I thought I was a stronger Christian than this. Most of the time I don't even know what to say to Bonnie. I just have to trust that the Lord forgives me and that Bonnie has forgiven me also.

Bonnie: I know that the Lord has forgiven you and I am working really hard because the Lord asks us to forgive as we are ourselves forgiven but sometimes Arthur I just don't even feel like I know who you are or what you stand for. I don't understand how you could do this to us?

Therapist: Bonnie, I hear that there is a real struggle for you, between your desire to forgive and the anger that you feel about this betrayal.

The couple's Christian theology utilized the discourse that forgiveness was the expected first act from Bonnie which contributed to her inner conflict and stifled Arthur from experiencing his shame. Revealing hidden discourses around an expectation of forgiveness that stifled and caused conflict versus a relational forgiveness grounded in mutual authenticity was essential to their healing. It became an important area of healing in therapy that Arthur expresses his full range of authentic guilt and shame just as critically as Bonnie needed to express her authentic anger. Uncovering these gendered and Christian discourses that hid her emotional expression (i.e., that meekness is an important trait for a Christian woman) was also central in setting the stage for mutual healing.

Creating an equitable foundation was also necessary for their spiritual healing. I explored Arthur's experience of guilt and shame and began to bring attention to his struggle to fully accept God's forgiveness: "I just have to trust the Lord forgives me. I expanded on Arthur's internal spiritual conflict as a way of exploring the paradox of two seemingly contradictory truths: forgiveness as both a moment and a process. Because of the couple's Christian world view, I drew on Bible verses to demonstrate that in a *moment* God had already forgiven Arthur (1 John 1:19), and it would be a *process* for Arthur to "leave his life of sin" (John 8:11) which included the impact of damaging his marital commitment. For therapists who may not desire to or are unable to quote scripture, asking clients to identify specific passages that help support the idea of forgiveness as a process can also be helpful. We discussed other supportive Bible passages to deepen this idea of forgiveness as both moment *and* process (e.g., the message *and* ministry of reconciliation in 2 Corinthians 5:18–19). Expanding their religious discourse to encompass Arthur's spiritual accountability further set the stage for the couple's relational and spiritual healing.

Phase II: Placing Infidelity in the Social and Religious Context

The goal in the second stage of affair work is to help the couple understand the relational effect of the social and religious context connected to the infidelity (Williams, 2011). This is done by reframing the affair within the larger social and religious context and making explicit the gendered power and religiously informed power processes associated with the infidelity (Williams, 2011). Reframing the affair within these larger contexts also helps partners experience the reality and implications of often invisible power imbalances.

I knew Bonnie and Arthur needed to engage in a thorough exploration of the underlying biblical-based assumptions, after which they worked to pattern their relationship. As I listened to these conversations, I was looking for those traditional discourses that highlight subtle power discrepancies within their union. Discrepancies often emerge in conversations about how couples organize around gendered household tasks, child care responsibilities, and financial spending. Different roles are not inherently problematic, but they become so when decision-making is unequal and embedded in imbalances due to a narrow construction of Christian male headship. Conversations that highlight "unfairness" often come up, and I have found unraveling the subtle organizing principles of inequality especially helpful. I should note I am careful not to debate my clients' theological assumptions or beliefs, but I do support them in beginning to question those feelings of "unfairness" as it relates to their often, gendered ways of interacting and Christian values.

This was pertinent for Bonnie, as a source of significant hurt for her revolved around the idea that her "repayment" for "years of service to Arthur" was his affair. Part of her discourse was that service to Arthur and their family was her duty as a Christian wife. For the majority of their marriage, Arthur had played the traditional role as provider, and they both viewed him as the spiritual leader and head of the home. These traditional Christian values led to a subtle power imbalance where Arthur's needs were prioritized over Bonnie's which continued in retirement and allowed him the privilege of "finding himself" and ultimately led to the opportunity for his affair. As spiritual leader he also had the "right" to invite whomever he pleased to church and their home, expecting that Bonnie provide the Sunday meal after such events. As Arthur and Bonnie began to understand how their structure related to a subtle imbalance over the years, the couple began to place the affair within a context that made sense to them.

Arthur was sincere in his desire to rectify both his "mistake around the affair" and to learn how to better serve his family. That meant that he became more open to exploring and understanding Bonnie's anger around the affair as well as his own privileged position within their marriage. They also directly began to challenge how they had understood their Christianity in relation to their marriage. Both were able to develop an expanded view of male headship that encompassed the concepts of what they called "servant leadership" which reflected more mutuality and equality though those terms were not used.

Phase III: Practicing Relational and Spiritual Mutuality

The goal in this third stage of recovery involves helping the couple experience new relational and spiritual possibilities beyond the infidelity (Williams, 2011). In order to do this, I had to help Bonnie and Arthur continue to define their personal meaning of equality and further explore those unscripted equalitarian ideals. We were then able to operationalize what equality and mutuality means so we could deepen the relational experiences of trust and connection that fosters movement toward forgiveness (Williams, 2011). For Arthur this meant starting to practice those aspects of "servant leadership" that had been discussed both in and out of session. For Bonnie, this meant continuing to foster her authentic voice, which included sharing feelings of anger and "unfairness." Much of the equality skill development for this couple meant they had to figure out how to engage in mutual vulnerability and relational responsibility.

Vulnerability For Arthur this was a new realization, as he discovered for the first time how invulnerable he had actually been throughout their marriage. Bonnie had a similar realization of withholding her emotions from Arthur; however, it was critically important they recognize that their invulnerability came from different power positions within their marriage. Arthur's position as head of the couple privileged his experience, feelings, and opportunities, and he unintentionally withheld those aspects of his life that made him vulnerable for fear of being seen as "weak" in this position. For Bonnie, her lack of vulnerability came from her own Christian discourse of meekness as well as a fear and sometimes a reality of not being heard or understood. For the majority of their marriage her anger over various things was dismissed both by her own religious script and Arthur's struggle to hear and validate her feelings. Thus, mutual vulnerability was a learning curve for both. As they practiced mutual vulnerability as a couple, we explored how they were also becoming more vulnerable in their spiritual life. For Arthur sharing feelings of "insecurity" and "weakness" with God in prayer reinforced these new behaviors of vulnerability in his marriage.

Relational Responsibility A second aspect of significant learning involved operationalizing and promoting a shared responsibility for relationship maintenance and each other's well-being. Their traditional-gendered power imbalances had dictated who responds to whom, with Bonnie in the role of caring for Arthur and their relationship. Arthur's affair provided a newfound motivation for them to learn a sense of relational responsibility. Bonnie had carried this responsibility almost entirely on her own over the 50 years of their marriage, and she was very accustomed to monitoring her behavior in relationship to Arthur's well-being. Arthur, on the other hand, had little sense of how things were going and still struggled post-affair to have a working knowledge of how Bonnie was on a daily basis. It became essential to ground relational responsibility as a Christian ideal and then support both Bonnie and Arthur in learning how to share this responsibility. Again, drawing on the script of servant leadership, Arthur was able to initiate conversations about Bonnie's well-being that opened the door for relationship maintenance work. Bonnie, on the other hand, had to work to allow Arthur space to pursue such conversations. This was hard at first, but as they practiced this in session, it became easier for Arthur to track Bonnie's well-being and for Bonnie to engage authentically. They were then able to reinforce these new skills as they applied relational responsibility in their prayer life. Rather than being a passive recipient of God's forgiveness, Arthur expanded his understanding of his relationship with God to include a more active participation in his spiritual growth and connection with God.

Implications for a Socially Just, Spiritually Integrated Practice

As we seek to understand how to integrate spiritual factors in affair recovery, it is important to keep in mind two essential elements involved in this process: (1) foster clinician spiritual integration and (2) separate harmful and healing influences. It is nearly impossible to help clients integrate their own spirituality if clinicians have not worked to integrate their own faith perspective in their therapeutic work. This can be a challenging process but is absolutely necessary prior to supporting clients in their own integration. Questions that may be helpful to consider include: (1) How does my faith influence my work? (2) What is my theology of suffering? (3) What role does prayer and/or faith play as a coping resource for myself or my clients? (4) What role does my faith play in my understanding of social justice issues and the structure of couple relationships? (5) What role does my faith play in my understanding of affairs? These questions are really a starting point to help uncover our own integration experience but are important elements of centering ourselves if we expect clients to integrate their spirituality as well.

Separating harmful and healing influences requires us to recognize those relational stances that work to hinder the development of intimacy and connection. One of the most organizing principles of this process is power dynamics, as inequalities impede the development of vulnerability and relational accountability. In an article entitled, Gendered Power, Spirituality, and Relational Processes: Experiences of Christian Physician Couples (2014), Esmiol Wilson, Knudson-Martin, and Wilson suggest that clinicians must "support relationally oriented gendered power-sharing and assess for gendered power inequality, focusing specifically on couple's directional dialogue, patterns of interactions, and emotional tones" (p. 333). Additionally, the authors advocate for clinicians to be aware of the link between spirituality and couple relationships and "consider spirituality as another form of relational interaction" (p. 334). Thus, helping clients unpack which aspects of their relational interactions, often fueled by underlying biblical assumptions that have never been processed, have a harmful versus helpful effect is key to separating these influences that affect their lives.

Conclusion

The integration of spirituality and social justice looks different for every couple across various social locations and life stages. It is therefore critical to be able to pull out the nuances of client's faith perspectives as these continue to organize their relational experiences for the betterment or determent of healing. Often, without a therapist acknowledgment of these faith perspectives, little reorganization or integration is able to occur; thus they continue to work toward the determent of affair recovery.

The beauty in crisis is that it has a priming effect for change, and many couples I have seen have been able to not only deepen and reorganize their relational experiences but with focused attention in treatment have been able to deepen their faith and understanding of God in the process. "Consider it pure joy, my brothers and sisters, whenever you face trials of many kinds, because you know that the testing of your faith produces perseverance. Let perseverance finish its work so that you may be mature and complete, not lacking anything" (James 1: 2–4).

References

Atkins, D. C., Baucom, D. H., & Jacobson, N. S. (2001). Understanding infidelity: Correlates in a national random sample. *Journal of Family Psychology, 15*, 735–749.

Brown, E. (2005). Split self affairs and their treatment. In F. Piercy, K. Hertlein, & J. Wetchler (Eds.), *Handbook of clinical treatment of infidelity* (pp. 55–69). New York: Routledge.

Esmiol Wilson, E. (2018). From assessment to activism: Utilizing a justice-informed framework to guide spiritual and religious clinical interventions. In E. Esmiol Wilson & L. A. Nice (Eds.), *Socially just religious and spiritual interventions: Ethical uses of therapeutic power, AFTA Springer Briefs*. Cham, Switzerland: Springer.

Esmiol Wilson, E., Knudson-Martin, C., & Wilson, C. (2014). Gendered power, spirituality, and relational processes: Experiences of Christian physician couples. *Journal of Couple & Relationship Therapy, 13*, 312–338. https://doi.org/10.1080/15332691.2014.953652

Fife, S. T., Weeks, G. R., & Stellberg-Filbert, J. (2011). Facilitating forgiveness in the treatment of infidelity: An interpersonal model. *Family Therapy*. https://doi.org/10.1111/j.1467-6427.2011.00561.x

Glass, S. P. (2003). *Not just friends: Rebuilding trust and recovering your sanity after infidelity*. New York: Free Press.

Goldner, V. (1985). Feminism and family therapy. *Family Process, 24*, 31–47.

Hare-Mustin, R. T. (1978). A feminist approach to family therapy. *Family Process, 17*, 181–194.

Knudson-Martin, C., & Mahoney, A. (Eds.). (2009). *Couples, gender, and power: Creating change in intimate relationships*. New York: Springer.

Lammers, J., Stoker, J., Jordan, J., Pollmann, M., & Stapel, D. (2011). Power increases infidelity among men and women. *Psychological Science*, 221–227. https://doi.org/10.1177/0956797611416252

Moultrup, D. (2005). Undercurrents. In F. Piercy, K. Hertlein, & J. Wetchler (Eds.), *Handbook of clinical treatment of infidelity* (pp. 31–40). New York: Routledge.

Olmstead, S., Blick, R., & Mills, L. (2009). Helping couples work toward the forgiveness of marital infidelity: Therapist's perspectives. *The American Journal of Family Therapy, 37*, 48–66.

Snyder, D. K., Baucom, D. H., & Gordon, K. C. (2007). Treating infidelity: An integrative approach to resolving trauma and promoting forgiveness. In P. Peluso (Ed.), *Infidelity: A practitioner's guide to working with couples in crisis* (pp. 99–125). Philadelphia: Routledge.
Snyder, D. K., & Doss, B. D. (2005). Treating infidelity: Clinical and ethical directions. *Journal of Clinical Psychology, 61*, 1453–1465.
Treas, J., & Giesen, D. (2000). Sexual infidelity among married and cohabitating Americans. *Journal of Marriage and the Family, 62*, 48–60.
Weeks, G. R., Gambescia, N., & Jenkins, R. E. (2003). *Treating infidelity: Therapeutic dilemmas and effective strategies*. New York: W.W. Norton.
Williams, K. (2011). A socio-emotional relational framework for infidelity: The relational justice approach. *Family Process, 50*, 516–528.
Williams, K., Galick, A., Knudson-Martin, C., & Huenergardt, D. (2012). Toward mutual support: A task analysis of the relational justice approach to infidelity. *Journal of Marital and Family Therapy*. https://doi.org/10.1111/j.1752-0606.2012.00324
Williams, K., & Knudson-Martin, C. (2012). Do therapists address gender and power in infidelity: A feminist analysis of the treatment literature. *Journal of Marital and Family Therapy*. https://doi.org/10.1111/j.1752-0606.2012.00303.x.14

Chapter 8
Finding a Way Through: Integrating Spirituality and Sociocultural Meaning in the Face of Infertility and Perinatal Loss

Lana Kim and Elisabeth Esmiol Wilson

Decisions around family building are deeply personal, and there are many avenues that individuals and couples can explore for establishing a family unit. Individuals or couples can bring children into their lives by fostering, closed or open adoption, embryo adoption, sperm donation, egg donation, surrogacy, or through marriage with stepchildren. Others have children in the symbolic sense through their chosen families. Yet, there are also many who desire to have a bloodline family.

Obstacles to Conception and Bloodline Parenthood

Many who desire a bloodline family face unexpected obstacles. According to the Centers for Disease Control (CDC), infertility affects approximately 12% of women and at least 9% of men (https://www.cdc.gov/reproductivehealth/infertility/index.htm). Infertility is the inability to conceive and have a successful live birth after 12 months of trying or 6 months for women 35 years and older (Zegers-Hochschild et al., 2009). Infertility also encompasses perinatal loss which refers to miscarriage, stillbirth, and early neonatal death. There is a growing need for family therapists who are trained to work with those affected by infertility and perinatal loss.

L. Kim (✉)
Department of Counseling Psychology, Lewis & Clark College, Portland, OR, USA
e-mail: lkim@lclark.edu

E. Esmiol Wilson
Marriage and Family Therapy Program, Pacific Lutheran University, Tacoma, WA, USA
e-mail: esmiolev@plu.edu

E. Esmiol Wilson, L. Nice (eds.), *Socially Just Religious and Spiritual Interventions*,
AFTA SpringerBriefs in Family Therapy, https://doi.org/10.1007/978-3-030-01986-0_8

Complex Intersections of Spirituality and Grief with Infertility and Perinatal Loss

Infertility and perinatal loss are some of the most profound losses that one can experience. These experiences can impact a person psychologically, emotionally, relationally, and spiritually (e.g., Cacciatore, DeFrain, & Jones, 2008; Kersting & Wagner, 2012; Lang et al., 2011). In addition to supportive relationships, religion and spirituality are cited as potential sources of support in preventing the development of complicated grief, PTSD, and psychiatric issues (e.g., Penzias, Dusek, & Merari, 2005; Roudsari, Allan, & Smith, 2007). Yet, injuries can also occur when pathologizing religious messages surrounding infertility or perinatal trauma are received and internalized. One can feel spiritual disillusionment, betrayal, or guilt which can lead people to question or reject their religious beliefs, values, and sense of spirituality (Romeiro, Caldeira, Brady, Hall, & Timmins, 2017).

This chapter will discuss the interconnections among sociocultural discourses about motherhood, gender and patriarchy, and religion and spirituality as they relate to treating infertility and perinatal trauma in therapy. In this chapter, religion refers to specific traditions, doctrines, and practices in contrast to spirituality which extends beyond religious doctrinal definitions and focuses on personal hopes, beliefs, and meanings in transcendent powers (Romeiro et al., 2017).

As two female authors, we bring personal experiences related to conception and infertility along with friends' and family members' stories of infertility and perinatal loss. We both have clinical interest and experience in working with families struggling with the intersections among religion, spirituality, infertility, and perinatal loss. We will each present a case example based on our own clinical experiences that demonstrates aspects of the relational, justice-informed framework (Esmiol Wilson, 2018) from Chap. 1, to help clients navigate these issues. The goal of clinical interventions will be twofold: (1) to counter harmful spiritual beliefs and sociocultural messages surrounding causation, regret, guilt, and blame related to infertility and perinatal loss and (2) to demonstrate how religion and spirituality can be used to support individuals and couples in finding acceptance and constructing personal meaning in the experience of grief and loss.

Infertility and Perinatal Loss as Disenfranchised Grief and Ambiguous Loss

In the United States, conception is still privileged through the dominant framework of heteronormativity, and we assume that it is a biological process that readily occurs for all. The pervasive nature of these societal assumptions obscures the reality for many including those that inhabit varying intersections of identity including ethnicity, gender identity, sexual orientation, religion, and socioeconomic class. This creates invisibility and stigma around infertility and perinatal loss and compounds it for persons who already experience marginalization because of their identities. For instance, lesbian infertility is often entirely unacknowledged or excluded within medical systems and societal discourses that privilege heteronormativity (Donovan, 2008). Furthermore, outside of medical communities, we tend to overlook the extent to which infertility is experienced by the general population, and even when there is acknowledgment, we struggle to bring it into our conversations. For those who struggle with infertility or have experienced perinatal loss, a type of ambiguous loss, the invisibility and societal minimization play a role in the construction of disenfranchised grief (Lang et al., 2011). There is a lack of recognition for losses constituting "what one never fully had."

Society at large struggles to acknowledge that the loss of a child in the context of pregnancy or perinatal loss can be as emotionally and psychologically intense as the loss of an older child (Lang et al., 2011). The meaning of the physical loss is often delegitimized or dismissed because there are few to no memories of the life that was lived which is often what is mourned or memorialized when a person dies. Infertility and perinatal loss include symbolic losses of hopes and dreams for the child, identity and envisioned role as parents, and the picture of a family unit. The intangible nature of these losses is often what makes it difficult for others to acknowledge, understand, and validate (Leon, 2008).

Constructions of Motherhood Through the Lens of Infertility and Perinatal Loss

The oppressive influence of patriarchy affects women and their experiences of infertility and perinatal loss. This is in part because in many societies, women are valued for their physical appearance and role as caregivers and mothers. Motherhood is powerfully shaped through a societal lens that enables men's voices to determine women's legitimacy and define women's realities. Yet, despite feminist movements that resist these single-story definitions of femininity and womanhood and claim women's rights to embody and enact their multiplicitous selves beyond the way they are seen through patriarchy, those who do not carry the title of mother may experience societal stigmatization and be viewed as less than (Romeiro et al., 2017).

Furthermore, dominant discourses continue to prescribe a set of criteria for what constitutes a "real" mother (i.e., the requirement to conceive and have a successful live birth). This challenges the "realness" of mothers who adopt or parent through any non-biological means. Ableism also delegitimizes mothers who experience perinatal loss and thus do not have living offspring to qualify their status and membership as mothers. This raises important questions about how mothers who experience these losses reconcile their identity and negotiate their affiliative membership in womanhood (Prinds, Hvidt, Mogensen, & Buus, 2014).

Guilt and Blame

Though women may resist these oppressive societal discourses by constructing their own standards and definitions of motherhood, women are not absolved from the deficit laden judgments of others in their immediate and larger contexts. Mothers are societally guilted and blamed in relationship to their children and specifically judged when they act out or are injured. Women who experience infertility and perinatal loss are also blamed. Women often feel that the loss and childlessness are due to their action, inaction, or inability. They wonder what they did, did not do, failed to do, or missed, and therefore, see themselves as primarily if not solely accountable. Societal blame compounds personal blame.

Blame and guilt can also be experienced in relation to delaying motherhood and planning for children at an advanced maternal age, typically defined as 35 years of age and older (Cunningham & Cunningham, 2013). Due to shifts in the cultural zeitgeist of our western society, the media as well as larger social messages suggest that childbearing can be postponed to one's late 30s or 40s, after a woman has had the opportunity to pursue an education, career, financial success, and other personal goals. However, conception during advanced maternal age is often a tenuous reality even with advances in ART. For women who experience involuntary childlessness and infertility related losses, the blame, shame, and guilt can be overwhelming.

Intersections of Religion and Spirituality with Infertility and Perinatal Loss

The process from pregnancy to delivery has been conceptualized as a spiritual one, even for nonreligious persons (Callister & Khalaf, 2010). In many societies, it is viewed as a sacred rite of passage (Prinds et al., 2014) or means of self-actualization and one that touches on existential issues of self-identity. The intersection between infertility and perinatal loss and religion and spirituality is complex. It can lead to spiritual suffering or spiritual crises where individuals or couples may question their beliefs, purpose, and meaning in life (Roudsari, Allan, & Smith, 2007).

The journey through infertility and ART can be uncertain. People may feel that their bodies are deficient or broken and feel betrayed by them. They may also experience a diminished sense of self and feel like a failure (Toscano & Montgomery, 2009). They may wrestle with questions of "why" and experience helplessness which creates a sense of hopelessness and despair. Religiously informed thoughts or beliefs can lead to additional questions such as: "Is God punishing me?" "Why is God betraying me?" "Is my faith not strong enough?" "Am I not good enough?" "What did I do to deserve this?" "Is this God's plan? It's not fair."

Relational Injuries Related to Religion and Spirituality

Religious messages abound regarding why couples might be infertile and how they should respond. For example, well-meaning, religiously embedded comments such as "pray more," "be patient and have faith," "if you believe and trust in Him, it will happen," and "God has a plan for your life" can feel insensitive and inadvertently blaming and dismissive. As noted in the first chapter, such harmful religious beliefs, commonly encountered in relation to experiences with infertility, can have detrimental effects on individual and couple mental health (Esmiol Wilson, 2018). It can create a sense of separation from one's religious community or relationship with God. Religious communities that highly value childbearing (e.g., "be fruitful and multiply") can further ostracize and stigmatize those experiencing infertility and perinatal trauma (Domar et al., 2005). In addition, religious doctrine regarding the use of medical intervention (e.g., the Catholic Church's Donum Vitae or "Gift of Life" which permits assisting the marital union, not replacing the procreative act) may be supportive for some but confining and isolating for others.

Therapeutic Challenges to Integrating Religion and Spirituality

Amidst confusion and pain, the journey through infertility and perinatal trauma can also offer an opportunity to revision and recreate meanings, purposes, and ways to fulfill one's life (Boivin et al., 2012). These painful experiences can become spiritually transformative (Peters, Jackson, & Rudge, 2011). However, therapeutic guidelines often lack clarity about how to integrate the spiritual dimension (Romeiro et al., 2017). It can be difficult to address spiritual issues for several reasons. For example, one's orientation around spirituality is deeply personal since it reflects a person's inner world, existential beliefs, world view, sense of moral and ethical center, faith in something bigger, and the values that matter to them most. As such, therapists often try to take careful measures to respect the uniqueness of each person's spiritual beliefs. However, sometimes the efforts to show respect for a client's spirituality create an awkwardness and sense of anxiety around how to bring issues of faith into conversation.

When religion and spirituality also represent an area of relational injury, hurt, or rejection, it can be even more difficult to know how and when to address it in the therapeutic process. Furthermore, family therapists can struggle to bring in the religious or spiritual dimension depending on where they are with it in their own lives. Processing self-of-the-therapist issues related to personal religious and/or spiritual experiences and seeking additional training, supervision, or consultation on integrating spirituality into treatment are recommended.

Interventions: Facilitating Spiritually Integrated Meaning-Making Processes

We offer four specific interventions and two extended case studies below that are embedded in the larger, ongoing, and recursive process of assessing, countering, and collaborating as described in Esmiol Wilson's (2018) justice-informed framework. We *assess* the client's role and relationship to spirituality and religion as it impacts experiences of infertility and perinatal loss. We ask questions from a place of curiosity to *counter* patterns of patriarchy, limiting societal discourses, internalization of self-blame, and experiences of spiritual harm. And we bring in a constructivist process to *support* new meaning-making and relational and spiritual connectedness.

Legitimize Loss in Its Spiritual and/or Religious Context

The literature on infertility and perinatal loss cites the buffering role that empathic care from medical providers, psychotherapeutic services, and social, emotional, and religious support systems can provide. These relationships can help prevent the development of complicated grief, PTSD, and psychiatric issues (Kersting & Wagner, 2012). Empathy involves validating and legitimizing the loss of infertility and perinatal trauma and giving space to grieve the reality of compounding losses. Linking these losses to one's faith and spirituality further legitimizes the pain while also opening possible avenues for healing.

Legitimize Relational Identity and Role as a Parent

Therapists can help counteract the detrimental effects of disenfranchised grief that one experiences when their status as mother is negated or delegitimized, by verbally acknowledging one's identity as mother even in the face of perinatal loss. It can also be meaningful to relate to the client and treat her as a *mother* who has experienced loss, rather than simply relating to her as a *woman* who has experienced loss. There is a therapeutic difference in naming such a woman a mother. Legitimizing this maternal identity plays an important role in co-constructing one's narrative around the loss and affirming the salience of one's self as mother.

Counter Harmful Religious Messages Embedded in Past or Current Faith Communities or Anti-religious Identities

Clients often report that they receive comments ranging from "pray more" or "God has a plan" to "this will all work out" or "don't worry, you'll get pregnant again" or even "be grateful God already blessed you with one healthy child." Whether our clients are aligned to certain religious or faith traditions or claim an anti-religious stance, as therapists, we need to not only be aware of but help counter these negative religious messages and how relationally and/or spiritually injurious they can be.

Renegotiate and Reconstruct Relationship with God or Faith in Something Bigger

As Esmiol Wilson's (2018) post-oppositional justice-informed framework suggests, part of countering the negative spiritual and religious messages surrounding infertility and perinatal trauma involves supporting positive and helpful expressions of faith. For individuals or couples who believe in a higher power or want to believe, facilitating a process of rebuilding faith can prove remarkably healing. A spiritual connection may feel tenuous at best after the waves of anger, grief, and disappointment related to unanswered prayers and feelings of spiritual abandonment. A therapist can inquire about a client's desire around deepening one's spiritual connection and explore what the client believes about how God or a higher power might feel about rebuilding that connection. In reconnecting, a client might need support to renegotiate a spiritual relationship that perhaps looks or feels different from their former connection.

Case Example #1: Maintaining Spiritual Connection Through Physical Loss

Sharon, a single, 37-year-old white, cisgender, heterosexual woman, came to see me (Lana) 6 months after she had lost her son at 28 weeks gestation. After 2 years and four failed intrauterine insemination (IUI) attempts, she got pregnant on her fifth cycle. Her loss came as unexpectedly as her pregnancy, and she was grappling with the reality that "it was over."

Legitimize Loss in Spiritual Context Although Sharon identified as an ex-Christian and someone who was currently non-religious, she likened her experience of infertility and pregnancy to a spiritual journey that had given her a sense of purpose and meaning. Losing her son, Brandon, in the final trimester did not make any sense to her. She could not understand what had gone wrong and wanted answers to "why?" She also felt a sense of despair as she grieved her hopes and dreams. In therapy, I (Lana) invited her to talk about the memories she had already created in her mind, ones that were already a part of her emotional reality: taking Brandon home, his first steps, first day of school, getting his driver's license, family camping trips, etc. By giving voice to the stories she had already begun to mentally write, we acknowledged the complexity of perinatal loss as more than just physical loss but ambiguous loss that is spiritual and relational and tied to an envisioned but unpenned future. We talked about how unfair it felt to grieve something she never got to experience.

Work in therapy involved naming and processing the anger, hurt, and senselessness of infertility and perinatal loss. We also related these to the disparate societal discourses around childbearing that make it difficult for people to know if, when, and how to pursue it. I facilitated therapeutic conversations that held the dialectical tensions between "this makes no sense" and "is there meaning in this," as well as "there is nothing to live for" and "how do I keep living in the face of this?" These therapeutic conversations enabled Sharon to explore existential concerns and reconcile what it looks like to move forward in the face of senseless loss and lost purpose.

Counter Harmful Religious Messages in Anti-religious Identity Sharon was struggling with feelings of guilt and self-blame. She wondered, like many do, questions such as, "Did I miss something?" "Could I have done something to prevent this?" "What should I have done that I did not do?" She understood the perinatal loss as a result of her inaction or failure. Many women ask these questions after perinatal loss, and I in part saw this as a reflection of the blame that society imposes on mothers for what happens to children, which mothers then internalize and take in as their own. In addition to the societal blame, Sharon had a long-standing relationship to self-blame which took stock in her life through childhood physical and emotional abuse by a fundamentalist Christian father who told her that she was the cause of his problems. Sharon stated that she had been deeply hurt by fundamentalist Christian beliefs that supported harmful enactments of patriarchy. She had been raised in a home where women and girls were supposed to be submissive to the male spiritual leader and head of home, responsible for the well-being of others, and taught that women were at fault for problems in the home.

Sharon saw Brandon's death as inherently her fault. In therapy, we deconstructed blame and processed the feelings of guilt associated with it. We spoke about the childhood trauma she endured as relational violations and reframed her self-blame as a learned response to a family system that had convinced her to serve as the container for blame. She grew to hold the stance that the blame she held was not hers to take on, and I supported her to feel and express the primary feeling of anger that she had been denied that undergirded her fear. Together we wondered whether Brandon's death was also not hers to own because it was outside of her mortality as a human to have prevented. As we unpacked the displaced blame and guilt and she let go of the blame that did not belong to her, she sobbed both feelings of sadness and relief.

Legitimize Relational Role as a Parent Few people in Sharon's familial, social, and societal world knew how to regard and relate to her around the perinatal loss. She felt identity-less. Thus, it was important to affirm Sharon's identity as a mother within a societal context that does not consider a person a mother until after birth when there is a child to qualify that status. The loss was also treated as a past event that she should get over. I legitimized her experience by saying, "I hear you expressing hurts from a mother's heart." By referring to her pain intentionally as a mother's pain, I was seeking to socio-emotionally attune to her affiliative membership as a mother. I was opening up space for remembering practices where emotional and relational connections could be maintained even in the face of physical death (Hedtke & Winslade, 2004). This proved to hold spiritual value for Sharon and offered her a way to explore transcendent meanings about life and purpose. Over the course of therapy, I helped Sharon co-construct deeper meanings about Brandon's presence in her life, what her relationship with Brandon was teaching her about herself, and how she could approach her future. Sharon expressed that these conversations instilled a sense of hope and faith in something bigger than her own visions for the possibilities of parenting.

Case Example #2: Renegotiating Service to God

A cisgender, white, middle-class Catholic couple in their late 20s came to see me (Elisabeth) after Josh became concerned that his wife Kathy's multiple miscarriages were the cause of her depression. The couple knew I was Protestant, not Catholic, but came to me because they hoped I would directly incorporate their faith and religious beliefs into treatment.

Legitimizing Religious Loss Through Reconnection with God Catholicism shaped this couple's world view and was an organizing force in their social and religious life. For Josh and Kathy, each miscarriage could only be understood in the larger context of God's plan. In therapy, legitimizing their loss meant validating their faith experience: "It sounds like while you know that some prayers are not answered and that God allows pain and suffering, it feels so raw and vulnerable to keep your heart open to God when you're hurting so much." Two months after I began working with this couple, Kathy was diagnosed with endometrial cancer and had to undergo a hysterectomy. As Catholics, this meant never having a biological child as they were theologically opposed to egg retrieval. Part of legitimizing this profound ambiguous loss included validating what they never had: "I see you both feeling the real loss of your shared dream of raising a large biological family in the Catholic church."

Another aspect included making room for new and uncomfortable feelings toward God. When I asked, "Can you share how you're feeling toward God?", Josh expressed, "For the first time I'm really angry at God, for taking all this away from us," while Kathy shared, "I just feel betrayed. I know God never betrays his people, but it just feels like he's taken too, too much." To fully legitimize the extent of their losses, I redirected them back to God: "What would it be like to share this with God? To tell him how you're really feeling?" For Josh and Kathy, God was a real presence in their life, and they needed to work out this grief with their God. I sometimes ask clients to engage with God through prayer exercises at home or journaling to God. Kathy preferred engaging with God in session as feelings were present.

Closing her eyes and silently praying in session, Kathy cried as she said aloud, "He knows, he knows how much this hurts and I just feel him holding me as I weep." Through such moments of reconnecting with God in their loss, this couple began experiencing moments of God's love and presence.

From Legitimizing Role as a Parent to Legitimizing Identity as Fruitful According to Catholic doctrine, the couple believed miscarriages are unborn babies, baptized by their explicit desire, and with God in heaven. However, Josh felt increasing comfort in trusting "God closed this door of biological children to us," while Kathy experienced a spiritual crisis. She had spent many years in Catholic high school and college discerning whether or not to enter a religious life. Her decision to marry Josh emerged as she felt "God's call" to service through the sacrament of marriage. Undergoing a hysterectomy before age 30 felt devastating at a spiritual level. "I thought God led me towards marriage. I thought His call on my life was motherhood, not barrenness. How do I understand all those religious experiences I had?" Rather than legitimizing their role as parents, something they already received through their faith, we began to unpack their understanding of parenthood in the larger context of fruitfulness. I asked, "so if God really did call Kathy to the sacrament of marriage, how do you both understand your vows in this unexpected place of barrenness?" For the couple, the sacrament of marriage held incredible significance. Guiding them to return to their beliefs regarding God's plan for marriage allowed Kathy to start healing. Rereading their church doctrine, they found incredible comfort in "trusting God's grace to grant us a marriage that radiates a fullness of charity, hospitality, and sacrifice." I supported Josh and Kathy in starting to dream about a new vision of their future, exploring different ideas about how they might serve God.

Reconstructing the Marital Relationship Through Respecting Spiritual Differences We terminated therapy only to have Josh call me several months later worried about Kathy, a similar pattern to how he first initiated therapy. In couple therapy, Kathy described that her grief over her "barrenness" would periodically emerge, unsettling Josh and causing him to worry about Kathy's faith in God's new plan for their lives. I helped Josh explore his feelings of inadequacy and tell Kathy how he struggled to see her in pain. I empowered Josh by helping Kathy share with him that "you being with me in my pain and not doubting my faith is the biggest form of support you can give me." As Josh began to legitimize Kathy's periodical reemergence of grief, she was increasingly able to feel valued for her vulnerability and emotionally connected relationship with God.

References

Boivin, J., Domar, A. D., Shapiro, D. B., Wischmann, T. H., Fauser, B. C. J. M., & Verhaak, C. (2012). Tackling burden in ART: An integrated approach for medical staff. *Human Reproduction, 27*, 941–950.

Cacciatore, J., DeFrain, J., & Jones, K. (2008). When a baby dies: Ambiguity and stillbirth. *Marriage and Family Review, 44*(4), 439–454.

Callister, L. C., & Khalaf, I. (2010). Spirituality in childbearing women. *The Journal of Perinatal Education, 19*, 16–24.

Cunningham, N., & Cunningham, T. (2013). Women's experiences of infertility – towards a relational model of care. *Journal of Clinical Nursing, 22*, 3428–3437.

Domar, A. D., Penzias, A., Dusek, J. A., Magna, A., Merari, D., Nielsen, B., et al. (2005). The stress and distress of infertility: Does religion help women cope? *Sexuality Reproduction and Menopause, 3*(2), 45–51.

Donovan, C. (2008). 'It's not really seen as an issue, you know, lesbian infertility it's kind of "what's that?"': Lesbians' unsuccessful experiences of medialized donor insemination. *Medical Sociology, 3*(1), 15–24.

Esmiol Wilson, E. (2018). From assessment to activism: Utilizing a justice-informed framework to guide spiritual and religious clinical interventions. In E. Esmiol Wilson & L. A. Nice (Eds.), *Socially just religious and spiritual interventions: Ethical uses of therapeutic power, AFTA Springer Briefs*. Cham, Switzerland: Springer.

Hedtke, L., & Winslade, J. (2004). *Re-membering lives: Conversations with the dying and the bereaved*. New York: Baywood Publishing Company.

Kersting, A., & Wagner, B. (2012). Complicated grief after perinatal loss. *Dialogues in Clinical Neuroscience, 14*(2), 187–194.

Lang, A., Fleiszer, A. R., Duhamel, F., Sword, W., Gilbert, K. R., & Corsini-Munt, S. (2011). Perinatal loss and parental grief: The challenge of ambiguity and disenfranchised grief. *Journal of Death & Dying, 63*(2), 183–196.

Leon, I. (2008). Helping families cope with perinatal loss. *The Global Library of Women's Medicine*. Retrieved online 26 Oct 2017. http://www.glowm.com/index/html?p=glowm.cml/section_view&articleid=417

Penzias, A., Dusek, J. A., & Merari, D. (2005). The stress and distress of infertility: Does religion help women cope? *Sexuality, Reproduction and Menopause, 3*(2), 45–51.

Peters, K., Jackson, D., & Rudge, T. (2011). Surviving the adversity of childlessness: Fostering resilience in couples. *Contemporary Nurse, 40*, 130–140.

Prinds, C., Hvidt, N. C., Mogensen, O., & Buus, N. (2014). Making existential meaning in transition to motherhood – a scoping review. *Midwifery, 30*, 733–741.

Romeiro, J., Caldeira, S., Brady, V., Hall, J., & Timmins, F. (2017). The spiritual journey of infertile couples: Discussing the opportunity for spiritual care. *Religion, 8*(76), 1–14.

Roudsari, R. L., Allan, H. T., & Smith, P. A. (2007). Looking at infertility through the lens of religion and spirituality: A review of the literature. *Human Fertility, 10*, 141–149.

Toscano, S. E., & Montgomery, R. M. (2009). The lived experience of women pregnant (including preconception) post in vitro fertilization through the lens of virtual communities. *Health Care for Women International, 30*, 1014–1036.

Zegers-Hochschild, F., Adamson, G. D., Mouzon, J., Ishihara, O., Mansour, R., Nygren, K., et al. (2009). The International Committee for Monitoring Assisted Reproductive Technology (ICMART) and the World Health Organization (WHO) revised glossary on ART terminology. *Human Reproduction, 24*, 2683–2687.

Chapter 9
Finding the Hidden Resiliencies: Racial Identity and Spiritual Meaning in Transracial Adoption

Brenda Rogers and Lindsey Nice

Transracial adoption (TRA) has a long history of controversy centering around whether White families, regardless of how well-intentioned, can prepare children of color to navigate a racist society. This can be further complicated when White parents are part of religious organizations that have historically rejected members based on race and are adopting children of color. In this chapter, we will briefly explore the history of race and religion in the USA and the multilevel challenges of transracial adoption when specifically, White, Christian parents adopt Black children. Through a case example, we will describe ways to (1) use therapist transparency to model openness by addressing issues of similarity and difference; (2) explore the racial and religious contexts of all family members; (3) increase more powerful family members' accountability through awareness of differences, including separating intent from impact; and (4) eschew a "one-size-fits-all" or "color-blind" approach for a socially just model that meets the specific spiritual and racial needs of each family member.

Introduction of Self

I (Brenda) have a master's degree in Marriage and Family Therapy and a postgraduate certificate in Therapy with Foster and Adoptive Families. In addition to my private practice, I am actively working with staff at my children's public elementary school to improve equity and racial/cultural awareness in education. I grew up in a rural farming community, going to the Methodist church, and not having much

B. Rogers (✉)
Rogers Family Counseling, Federal Way, WA, USA

L. Nice
Marriage and Family Therapy Program, Pacific Lutheran University, Tacoma, WA, USA

E. Esmiol Wilson, L. Nice (eds.), *Socially Just Religious and Spiritual Interventions*, AFTA SpringerBriefs in Family Therapy, https://doi.org/10.1007/978-3-030-01986-0_9

exposure to people of diverse ethnic backgrounds. My transition from being a single, White woman to becoming a half of a biracial couple, member of a large Black family, transracial adoptive mom, and parent to our two children of color has been enlightening, humbling, and painful – sometimes all at once. I've learned that my White privilege sneaks in when I don't expect it, even now, and that it shows up everywhere, including in the *years* that it took us to find a Christian church that felt safe and comfortable for all of us. I (Lindsey) am an assistant professor in the marriage and family therapy program at Pacific Lutheran University where Brenda completed her master's degree. I identify as a 33-year-old White, middle-class, heterosexual, cisgender woman, married with no children, and a third-generation Seventh-day Adventist.

Guiding Theories and Definitions

The theories that guide our work with transracial adoptive families include systems theory, which tells us that influencing one part of the system influences every part of the system, and feminist theory, which helps us to address the ways race, religion, social class, gender, and other identities frame our world views. In our clinical work with clients, we are additionally guided by critical race theory, which supports us in looking carefully at how race is constructed and the impact this has on relationships. We use our "agent" identity (Neito, 2010) to actively counter racist messages that limit families' abilities to connect with and support one another. While there are many complexities to transracial adoption, for the purpose of this paper, we will be focusing on White, Christian parents adopting Black children.

History of Racism and Christianity in the USA

It is impossible to untangle early religious history from the history of racism in the USA. John Locke, often memorialized as one of the earliest defenders of religious liberty in America, wrote in the 1669 "Fundamental Constitution" of the colony of Carolina:

> Since charity obliges us to wish well to the souls of men, and religion ought to alter nothing in any man's civil estate or right, it shall be lawful for slaves, as well as others, to enter themselves, and be of what church or profession any of them shall think best, and therefore, be as fully members as any free man. But yet no slave shall hereby be exempted from that civil dominion his master hath over him, but be in all things in the same state and condition he was in before.

In other words, Black people were granted the right to faith practices, so long as this did not interfere with their servitude.

White slaveholders vigorously defended their rights to own slaves by pointing to the presence of slavery in the Bible as evidence of God's preferred social structure. Slaveholders cited Bible verses such as Ephesians 6:5, which reads, "Servants, be obedient to them that are your masters according to the flesh, with fear and trembling, in singleness of your heart, as unto Christ," and encouraged slaves to submit to them as evidence of religious devotion. One such slave, Nat Turner, ran away from his owner at 22 but returned a month later after receiving a spiritual vision calling him to accept his place as a slave. Later, Turner's religious convictions shifted, and he led a rebellion of slaves against their slaveholders in 1831. Turner was caught, tried, and hanged, causing state legislators to pass a new law requiring that White ministers be present at all Black religious services.

After slavery was officially outlawed, Biblical scripture continued to be used to support inequality through Jim Crow laws, where Whites could refuse to serve Black people, citing their "religious freedom." Private Christian schools were created, allowing White Christian children an alternative to racially integrated public schools. One such example was Christian-affiliated Bob Jones University, which excluded Black applicants completely until 1971 and then admitted them on condition that they were married so as to deter interracial dating. In 1975, the university continued to "deny admission to applicants engaged in an interracial marriage or known to advocate interracial marriage or dating" and had official rules for students explicitly prohibiting interracial dating or risk expulsion (Schultz, West, & MacLean, 1999, p. 30).

While most Christian institutions have since distanced themselves from these earlier positions, this presents a complicated dilemma in that retroactively disavowing these "revelations" calls into question current interpretations of God's will. Ubiquitous religiously based messages like "we're all God's children" promote a "color blindness" that furthers many White Christian people from seeing the historic and contemporary impact of racism. This presents significant challenges for White, Christian parents adopting children of color.

History of Transracial Adoption

Transracial adoption (TRA) is generally defined as an adoption of a child whose race and ethnicity are different from his or her adoptive parent(s). This includes children adopted internationally and domestically. In the USA, the great majority of conflict, attention, and research focus on White parents adopting children of color, particularly Black children. This is largely due to "concern for the identity development of transracial adoptees" (Malott & Schmidt, 2012, p. 384). The majority of research about identity development in transracial adoption focuses on racial, ethnic, and cultural aspects of development, not religion or spirituality. Yet in the USA, religious antiabortion messages and religious calls to "look after orphans" (James 1:27, NIV) significantly increased support for international and domestic TRA among White Evangelical, Mormon, and conservative Catholic families, churches, and agencies (Perry, 2014). Such messages from the pulpits helped spur on the large demand for adoptions, which was largely responsible for the peak in 2004 with the USA accounting for 51% of international adoptions (Selman, 2009).

There are many criticisms of transracial adoption, primarily centering around the capability of White parents to help prepare Black children for the realities of racism. In 1972, the National Association of Black Social Workers (NABSW) released their "stand against the placement of Black children in White homes for any reason" (NABSW, 1972, p. 1), stating "The affirmation of our ethnicity promotes our opposition to the transracial placements of Black children" (NABSW, 1972, p. 1). They highlighted the value of community connections and the importance of learning coping strategies to deal with oppression, racism, and "White racism," including the "would you want your daughter to marry one syndrome" (NABSW, 1972, p. 3). It also calls out transracial adoption as "an expedient for White folk, not as an altruistic humane concern for Black children" (NABSW, 1972, p. 2).

Religion and Spirituality as Unsupportive in Transracial Adoption

While there is a fairly wide body of research showing that spiritual connection adds hope, resilience, and community across many cultural groups, religion has also been used as a disguise for the dominant group to maintain power. Some transracial adoption scholars have linked conservative Christian religious groups and their growing support for transracial adoption as a cover for years of political agendas (Perry, 2014). In other words, transracial adoption provides a convenient, altruistic solution for decreasing abortion, saving poor children of color, relieving the government from having to subsidize poor families, and continuing to marginalize people of color (Perry, 2014; Raible, 2015). Such agendas further fuel the polarizing views around transracial adoption, race, religion, and politics.

Research also indicates that religious parents are more likely to downplay race and have concerns about over-sensitizing children to race (Crolley-Simic & Vonk, 2011). Conservative Christian religious groups are specifically associated with practicing more "color-blind" techniques in their parenting and less culturally and racially sensitive support of transracial adoption (Lee, Vonk, & Crolley-Simic, 2015; Perry, 2014). Themes such as "God loves all children" or "We are all the same race—the human race" promote a color-blind approach in which all are seen as Children of God before anything else. While a common and well-intentioned approach, downplaying the impact of race has serious, lifelong implications for children of color who are unprepared and unsupported in the face of racism (Barn, 2013; Donaldson, 2008; Marr 2011; McRoy & Griffin, 2012).

Religion and Spirituality as Supportive in Transracial Adoption

When faith communities support the unique needs of transracial families, spirituality is directly correlated with improved adoption satisfaction for both children and their parents (Belanger, Copeland, & Cheung 2008; Gillum & O'Brien, 2010). Gillum and O'Brien (2010) researched Black adopted children and found spirituality and family support to be "protective factors for children who have endured adversity" (p. 1661). Children in their study showed that those with more spirituality and a belief in a "Greater Power who has their best interests at heart" were "less likely to allow negative events to dominate their lives" (Gillum & O'Brien, 2010, p. 1661). They also found that family support was crucial in helping children to strengthen their trust and feel a great sense of security (Gillum & O'Brien, 2010).

Similarly, research shows adoptive parents experience greater parenting satisfaction, less parental stress, and more feelings of support when holding a strong spiritual connection in a supportive faith organization (Belanger et al., 2008). For example, parents who described their faith in God as both central and essential in their adoption decision reported lower-than-average stress levels despite having children with extreme behavior challenges (Belanger et al. 2008). Adoptive parents with an intrinsic religiousness, or a strong religious world view, held a stronger level of religious commitment and less prejudicial views and were more altruistic in their reasons for adopting children (Howell-Moroney, 2014).

While religious and nonreligious parents have "similar levels of racial awareness" (Lee et al., 2015, p. 54), some parents report that church provides cultural socialization opportunities for their transracial family and that God guides them in "decisions about helping their children cope with potential racism" (Lee et al., 2015, p. 43). Studies support these socialization efforts and show that relationships with same-race peers neutralize negative emotional experiences of discrimination and establish positive connections to their race and culture (Huh & Reid, 2000; Padilla, Vargas, & Chavez, 2010). Involvement in a faith community with a large transracial adoption or diverse community can be an ideal opportunity for growth in spiritual, racial, and cultural identity development.

Case Study

In this case study, I (Brenda) will describe a contextually sensitive systemic-feminist approach (Esmiol Wilson, 2018) to integrating religion and spirituality into therapy with a transracial adoptive family. Specific clinical benchmarks include (1) using therapist transparency to model openness by addressing issues of similarity and difference between myself as the therapist and clients; (2) explicitly exploring the racial and religious contexts of all family members; (3) increasing more powerful family members' accountability through awareness of differences, including separating intent from impact; and (4) eschewing a "one-size-fits-all" or "color-blind" approach for a supportive model that meets the specific spiritual and racial needs of each family member.

Lisa (47, White) and her husband, John (47, White), adopted Keira (14, Black) as an infant through an open adoption with a private, Christian adoption agency. Lisa and John additionally had one biological child, Tyler (18), with whom Keira has historically been close. Lately there had been tensions, which the parents attributed to Keira emotionally pulling away from friends and family. In addition to retreating from her family and friends, Lisa and John had noticed Keira quitting hobbies she'd previously enjoyed and struggling academically. Their assumption was that she was "depressed," and they wondered if this was "an adoption thing."

Using Therapist Transparency

In my initial joining with Lisa, John, Keira, and Tyler, I met with them separately (parents, parents and Tyler, Keira, and then together) over the first few sessions. This allowed for open conversations about their experiences pre- and post-adoption without worry that parents or children would be offended or burdened with difficult details or opinions. It also provided me valuable insight into potential layers of contributing factors in adoption, such as loss and grief (includes parental fertility issues), traumatic events, attachment issues, guilt and shame, fears of disloyalty or rejection, fears of exposing secrets, identity challenges, and the like.

In these sessions, I used the ADDRESSING model (Hays, 2008) to facilitate exploration of our different contexts, including race, gender, social class, and more. We talked about how each person locates themselves in different areas of the model and how similarities or differences between myself, as the therapist, and each family member had the potential to affect our conversations going forward. I asked questions like, "I wonder what you think I might get, or not get, about your experience because I haven't experienced it myself (i.e. because I'm White, or because I'm not adopted)?" and "What would be helpful for me to know about what it's been like to be you?" Sharing my own intersecting identities helped set the tone for therapy in which we regularly, explicitly talk about the ways context impacts our lived experiences.

Exploring Racial and Religious Contexts

When I asked how race impacts their family, John and Lisa replied that they "don't think about it much" and that they "don't want Keira to feel different than anyone else." My layered response as the therapist was first to (1) recognize that their lack of attention to race was impacted by much larger, oppressive discourses about race, (2) validate the fear underlying the misguided though well-meaning, religiously informed intentions of the parents ("You want her to feel included, you don't ever want her to feel different"), and then (3) approach connecting their "color blindness" to the larger racial discourse with curiosity ("You know, that's a really common thought – that if we talk about differences, it will somehow further the distance between us. I wonder where that idea comes from: that we shouldn't talk about this difference of race between you?").

Lisa talked about her experience of growing up in an Evangelical home where she routinely heard the message "all are precious in His sight." She remembered being hushed by her mother in a grocery store as a child when she pointed out how dark another person's skin was. John said in his Catholic home, they "didn't see race," and in therapy, we talked about where that idea originated. We talked about White churches and White discomfort with naming White privilege and the unintended but nevertheless harmful use of White privilege to avoid seeing inequality by hiding behind spiritual truths (all made in God's image). At that point, I wasn't sure if it would be furthering Keira's vulnerable position to ask her to reflect on this, so I posed the question: "I don't want you to feel like you need to answer right now, but I wonder what it's like for you, Keira, to hear that? I wonder if it's comforting in ways, or if it discounts some of your experiences, or maybe it's something else completely."

Increasing Accountability

There was a visible shift in the room as Keira saw her parents reflecting on these "color-erasing" messages, often supported by their religious contexts. As I gently encouraged Keira's reflections on what it was like to hear them talk like this, she responded "It makes me feel less crazy." We talked further about the idea of "crazy," and Keira divulged details of her experiences at school and home that her parents had never heard before, such as the loneliness of being only one of two Black teens in her classes (her parents had previously described her school as "diverse"). All of these experiences shared a common thread of Keira feeling like the "other" in a sea of White – the exact thing her parents had hoped to protect her from by not acknowledging race. When asked where she felt safe and accepted, Keira replied that her church youth group was helpful: "When I'm at youth group, I just feel like one of the group. I fit in. There are other kids just like me ... they get it." Keira was referring to kids who had transracial adoption stories.

As we talked more about the youth group, Lisa mentioned that she'd worked hard to find a church with "families that look like ours." In fact, the family drove 40 min each way to attend this church in a neighboring city. This was the first time I'd heard either parent directly expresses actions they'd taken to soothe their worry that Keira might not fit in based on the color of her skin. I gently reflected back to

Lisa and John that "while you've been unintentionally using 'religious acceptance' to deflect important conversations about racial difference (and even issues like racism and oppression) it sounds like finding a religious community reflective of your family racial difference was very important to you." Additionally, I highlighted their inner resilience and strength to persist until they found a church reflective of their transracial family and for Keira to use her resilience and courage to give voice to her struggle against "otherness."

When I asked Keira, "What is it like to hear that they are worried about you not fitting in specifically because of your skin color?" she responded, "It feels good. I guess I never thought they noticed." I invited Lisa and John to build on their resilience and support for Keira's experience by starting to notice racial difference and talk to both Keira and Tyler about the impact of racial disparities. I encouraged the family to discuss in what ways their Christian faith might inform an active response to racial oppression. I also encouraged Lisa and John to ask Keira what else she might need them to know. Keira shared that she appreciated her mom's friendship with Auntie Tamra, a Black professional woman Lisa had been friends with for years, and that she also appreciated having contact with her birth family. Again, these highlighted the importance of connection to her racial, cultural, ethnic, and biological roots for Keira.

Establishing a More Socially Just, Supportive Model

By opening up a space to talk not only about racial differences but about racial injustices and oppression, Lisa, John, Keira, and Tyler were able to connect in new ways. No longer were issues of race off-limits, but rather they became a part of regular family discussions going forward. Keira's religious home was a healing space where she felt seen and understood by other children with their own transracial adoption stories. Rather than a one-size-fits-all or there-are-no-differences-between-us model, family members were able to share their unique experiences and support each other across difference.

Given their new awareness and ability to be transparent in courageous conversations, when Keira described microaggression from a student in her class, Lisa and John had new strategies for supporting Keira and Tyler. They helped Tyler learn that harassing this student online didn't help Keira any more than her parents ignoring race as the subtext of the student's comments. Instead Lisa and John named the student's White privilege, talked to both Keira and Tyler about the racism inherent in the microaggression, supported Keira in talking to her principal, and followed up with a parent meeting. The family was able to live in the complexity of these issues, understanding that religion could either perpetuate harmful ideas about ignoring difference or provide a supportive anchor for the family's core beliefs. Knowing this, they were able to center around their spiritual strengths and feel more authentically connected as a family.

Clinical Implications

While adoption is often celebrated as a way of bringing people together, it is built on loss. For a child to need a new family, they had to lose one. Many adoptive parents experience losses prior to adoption as well. It is important for therapists to recognize this and educate ourselves about the common factors of adoption. Transracial families often experience the same core issues as biological families, plus an intricate tapestry of pieces specific to experiences such as racism, marginalization, fear, isolation, etc. Many adoptive families, including transracial ones, are unaware of these complex issues and may appreciate support and education from therapists to help them normalize and understand their experiences. For these reasons, learning about each family's underlying past experiences and any unhelpful beliefs about themselves or biases about others (race, ethnicity, religion, bad birth families, etc.) is vital. Separating the family, especially in the initial two to three sessions, allows parents to talk about difficult truths in the adoption process, losses, and biases without their child hearing; children can also speak without feeling disloyal or increasing their vulnerability.

For families learning about their White privilege, noticing that they can't give their privileges to their children or shield them from its negative effects can leave them feeling helpless and trigger previous grief. Faith can play a significant role for many families in countering such negative feelings and helping them build their resilience and resolve to move forward. Therapists can encourage families to find supportive faith communities and non-faith communities, which have other transracial families who get it. Having a supportive community builds resilience and may also counter many of the negative experiences for both parents and children, especially for adopted children to see that they are not alone in their transracial experiences.

Conclusion

A holistic approach that understands religious as well as racial, ethnic, and cultural influences is crucial to helping transracial families and youth. Working within the transracial adoption community requires social justice advocacy in order to "empower families or youth to confront racism within the system or individuals who maintain the system" (Malott & Schmidt, 2012, p. 388). In some situations, "the system" may refer to religious organizations or aspects of a family's religious beliefs, which may further complicate spirituality in transracial adoption. Therapist's willingness to engage in these issues through self-reflection, transparency, and curious questioning can help to create space where difference is no longer ignored but instead where racial disparity and injustice are openly addressed so that each family members' individual and relational needs are better met.

References

Barn, R. (2013). 'Doing the right thing': Transracial adoption in the USA. *Ethnic and Racial Studies, 36*(8), 1273–1291. https://doi.org/10.1080/01419870.2013.770543
Belanger, K., Copeland, S., & Cheung, M. (2008). The role of faith in adoption: Achieving positive adoption outcomes for African American children. *Child Welfare, 87*(2), 99–123.
Crolley-Simic, J., & Vonk, M. E. (2011). White international transracial adoptive mothers' reflections on race. *Child & Family Social Work, 16*, 169–178.
Esmiol Wilson, E. (2018). From assessment to activism: Utilizing a justice-informed framework to guide spiritual and religious clinical interventions. In E. Esmiol Wilson & L. A. Nice (Eds.), *Socially just religious and spiritual interventions: Ethical uses of therapeutic power, AFTA Springer Briefs*. Cham, Switzerland: Springer.
Evan B. Donaldson Adoption Institute. (2008). *Finding families for African American children: The role of race & law in adoption from foster care: Policy & practice perspective*. New York: The Evan B Donaldson Adoption Institute.
Gillum, N., & O'Brien, M. (2010). Adoption satisfaction of Black adopted children. *Children and Youth Services Review, 32*, 1656–1663. https://doi.org/10.1016/j.childyouth.2010.07.005
Hays, P. (2008). *Addressing cultural complexities in practice*. New York: American Psychological Association.
Howell-Moroney, M. (2014). The empirical ties between religious motivation and altruism in foster parents: Implications for faith-based initiatives in foster care and adoption. *Religions, 5*, 720–737. https://doi.org/10.3390/rel5030720
Huh, N. S., & Reid, W. J. (2000). Intercountry, transracial adoption and ethnic identity: A Korean example. *International Social Work, 43*(1), 75–87.
Lee, J., Vonk, M. E., & Crolley-Simic, J. (2015). Religion and cultural and racial socialization among international transracial adoptive parents. *Journal of Social Distress and the Homeless, 24*(1), 40–57. https://doi.org/10.1179/1053078915z.00000000022
Malott, K., & Schmidt, C. (2012). Counseling families formed by transracial adoption: Bridging the gap in the multicultural counseling competencies. *The Family Journal: Counseling and Therapy for Couples and Families, 20*(4), 384–391. https://doi.org/10.1177/1066480712451231
Marr, E. (2011). "I'll have the melting pot soup with a side of Black:" Transracial adoption and the racial-ethnic color line. *Michigan Sociological Review, 25*, 33–52.
McRoy, R., & Griffin, A. (2012). Transracial adoption policies and practices: The US experience. *Adoption & Fostering, 36*(3–4), 38–49.
National Association of Black Social Workers. (1972). *National Association of Black Social Workers position statement on trans-racial adoptions*. New York: National Association of Black Social Workers.
Neito, L. (2010). *Beyond inclusion, beyond empowerment: A developmental strategy to liberate everyone*. Olympia, WA: Cuetzpalin.
Padilla, J. B., Vargas, J. H., & Chavez, H. L. (2010). Influence of age on transracial foster adoptions and its relation to ethnic identity development. *Adoption Quarterly, 13*, 50–73. https://doi.org/10.1080/10926751003662598
Perry, S. (2014). Conservative Christians and support for transracial adoption as an alternative to abortion. *Social Science Quarterly, 95*(2), 380–392.
Raible, J. (2015). Introduction to the special issue: Race, religion, and rescue in adoption. *Journal of Social Distress and the Homeless, 24*(1), 1–6.
Schultz, J. D., West, J. G., & MacLean, I. S. (1999). *Encyclopedia of religion in American politics* (Vol. 2). Santa Barbara, CA: Greenwood Publishing Group.
Selman, P. (2009). The rise and fall of intercountry adoption in the 21st century. *International Social Work, 52*(5), 575–594.

Chapter 10
Fostering Security: Spiritually Informed Attachment-Based Therapy for Infants and Caregivers

Lina S. Ponder

Infant Attachment Security, Parental Reflective Functioning, and God Image

This chapter begins with the assumption that attachment between individuals, families, and society is important and impacts parenting. For the purpose of this chapter, I will be describing a therapeutic spiritual formation group, in which clients self-selected to participate, and will be focusing on a Christian interpretation of God. In the group, we focus on clients' "God image," or way they see God as looking toward them (e.g., "I think God may be mad at me right now," "I know God is forgiving," "I'm afraid of God"), and connections between this and other points of relational and societal attachment in their lives. For my doctoral work, I suggested parental reflective functioning capacity (i.e., a caregiver's ability to understand and hold both her own and her child's actions and emotions) may be strengthened by accessing supportive God images. Here, I expand these ideas to include the importance of addressing larger contextual inequities and resulting insecure attachment to society when working with clients to counter unhelpful God images and access supportive God images. Simply stated, affirming ways that inequity has made parenting difficult and supporting clients in experiencing a more loving and compassionate view of God can help caregivers parent in preferred ways and strengthen attachment to children.

I identify as a biracial (Korean and Caucasian) 1.5 generation immigrant Christian woman. Spirituality is a central aspect of my identity and worldview. Diverse spiritual settings from my childhood in South Korea and the United Kingdom along with 10 years of my adulthood spent in African-American, Latino-American, and Chinese-American Christian faith communities taught me to be sensitive to cultural values

L. S. Ponder (✉)
Biola University, La Mirada, CA, USA
e-mail: lina.s.ponder@biola.edu

E. Esmiol Wilson, L. Nice (eds.), *Socially Just Religious and Spiritual Interventions*,
AFTA SpringerBriefs in Family Therapy, https://doi.org/10.1007/978-3-030-01986-0_10

embedded in one's faith practice. Spirituality may also profoundly affect individuals personally and be a central aspect of community identity in both helpful and harmful ways. A sizeable portion of my clinical practice is comprised of Christians who vary in their particular faith tradition background (e.g., Presbyterian, Catholic, Baptist, nondenominational). In my practice, there is a range in the role and level of current commitment my clients have to their faith communities, if any. For some, their felt sense of safety and belonging in a faith community has been compromised due to the reinforcement of negative beliefs and lack of support for the growing level of differentiation between the individual and their religious communities.

While attachment theory primarily focuses on the relationship between infants and caregivers (usually mothers), a systems perspective helps me to expand this to look at attachment between individuals, families, and society. Pamela Hays (1996) "ADDRESSING" model helps me to continue to look for ways in which we give unearned power to some and take away power from others. In addition, Leticia Nieto (2010) writes about "agent" (privileged) and "target" (marginalized) aspects of identity and supports me in having direct conversations with clients about ways they've experienced empowerment or disempowerment societally. Religion can span from supportive, in an environment where power, privilege, and context are taken into account and members actively work to dismantle inequity, to unsupportive, where difference is ignored and inequity is maintained.

I will illustrate in this chapter how I have integrated spirituality and an attention to larger contextual issues into caregiver interventions with what I call *Contemplative Focused Parenting* along with the *justice-informed framework for spiritual and religious resilience* (Esmiol Wilson, 2018).

Guiding Theories and Definitions

Attachment Bonds

While John Bowlby (1969/1982) developed the theory of attachment to explain the emotional connection between children and their caregivers, we now understand that humans can also experience attachment at the community and societal level. Secure attachment with a caregiver provides an emotional bond that improves a child's chance of survival. A social justice lens expands our understanding of secure attachment to include having a sense of belonging at the community and societal level. However, when caregivers experience societal sources of oppression, including disempowering religious discourses and practices, these unsafe social environments make a felt sense of safety and belonging different. Such attachment struggles at the societal level can deeply impact generations of caregivers and children, interrupting the experience of sensitivity, acceptance, and emotional availability necessary for a sense of connection and security. While features of secure attachment include flexible ability to explore from a place of safety and to seek comfort in relationship when one feels unsafe (Wallin, 2007, p. 12), such safety becomes illusory in an oppressive

Table 10.1 Attachment style categories

Attachment style	Characteristics	Caregiver style
Secure	Seek caregivers for comfort	Attuned to child's emotions and needs
Avoidant	Does not seek comfort from caregivers	Rejecting or unavailable
Ambivalent	Difficulty being consoled from caregivers	Inconsistent
Disorganized	Limited attachment behavior; confused and apprehensive with caregivers	Frightening to child; may be abusive or neglectful

Ainsworth, Blehar, Waters, and Wall (1978) and Main and Solomon (1990)

society. Religion can further reinforce such oppression through wielding a harsh and demanding God image. Or religion can counter such abuse through supporting an empowering and accepting God image (Table 10.1).

Implicit Relational Knowing

Karlen Lyons-Ruth (1998) and the rest of the Process of Change Study Group developed the construct of "implicit relational knowing" to better understand the mutually constructed emotion regulation pattern between persons. Similar to Bowlby's construct of the internal working model, it is this component of engagement with others that captures "how to be with someone" and how to gauge the meaning and following patterns of relationships (Lyons-Ruth et al., 1998, p. 284). This way of implicit knowing enters the infant's world before language skills are acquired and remains throughout life, usually beyond conscious awareness. As caregivers continue to make sense of and reflect back to infants their internal world, new ways of interaction continue to expand (Lyons-Ruth et al., 1998).

Parental Reflective Functioning

A caregiver's attachment style is believed to be passed down to their child through sensitive responsiveness (Ainsworth et al. 1978; Main & Solomon, 1990). Sensitivity is enhanced with parental reflective functioning which allows caregivers to comprehend one's own and others' behavior in light of underlying mental states (Slade, 2005). Mental states (intentions, feelings, thoughts, desires, goals, purposes, and beliefs) are used to make sense of and to anticipate one's and others' actions (Fonagy & Target, 1998). Too often, children are misunderstood when caregivers respond only to their behaviors and not to their mental states. Parents who are marginalized and disempowered have additional requirements asked of them: they must manage their own responses to constant pressures of racism, sexism, etc. while still attending to their children.

God Image

A person's cognitive understanding of God is known as their God concept (Grimes, 2007). Generally, God concepts are constructed by what we are taught about God from religious texts, spiritual leaders, and parents and capture how we feel toward God and our perception of how God may feel toward us (Grimes; Rizutto, 1979). God images are affect-laden representations that underlie a person's embodied, emotional experience with God and are primarily comprised of implicit relational knowledge (Thomas, Moriarty, Davis, & Anderson, 2011). Attachment theory provides a theoretical framework for understanding God images (Kirkpatrick, 1992). Just as infants develop an attachment to parents and parents develop an attachment to the larger society around them, individuals can also attach to an image of God. Therapists can work with clients to strengthen attachment at each of these levels in therapy: increasing parental reflective functioning, challenging oppressive societal messages, and helping clients to draw on a God image that is kind, forgiving, understanding, and just.

Interventions: Contemplative Focused Parenting

Building a caregiver's reflective stance and implementing God image interventions comprise the two main components of the principles of *Contemplative Focused Parenting*. I integrate this with my own focus on societal attachment and increasing families' sense of safety and connection to the world around them. These principles are informed from my own observations and current practices with clients, the Reflective Parenting Program (Slade, 2006), and Mindful Parenting (Reynolds, 2003). The therapist's big clinical focus is the enhancement of reflective capacity and deep empathy in verbal and nonverbal forms:

> This process is initiated through the parent developing an active observational stance, through the accumulated practice of directing quieted, patient, curious, alive attention to both child and self, and through learning to respect and follow the child's lead in contact-seeking and exploratory behaviors. (Reynolds, 2003, p. 362)

I begin by asking participants a variety of questions about their attachment to society, preferred parenting stances, and image of God.

Developing a Societal Attachment Perspective

- Ask directly about areas of context and identity, including ways in which clients are empowered and disempowered.
- Practice continued self-reflection on ways I am similar to or different than my clients and aspects of their experiences I may be prone to missing because of this.

- Invite conversation on how societal patterns of injustice (including through religion) have made it difficult for parents to practice parenting in preferred ways.
- Invite conversation on how parents have developed continued resilience because of experiences of injustice, and support preferred ways of parenting.

Developing a Parental Reflective Stance

- Slow down in order to create a reflective stance in order to notice moment-to-moment experiences.
- Reflect and help regulate caregiver mental states to them.
- Notice how increased resilience regarding larger religious/societal level oppression supports caregiver's regulation of mental states.
- Hold and voice the child's possible mental states underlying behavior.
- Gently reframe the child's behavior by verbalizing possible feelings underlying the behavior.
- Invite caregivers to consider the impact of their own thoughts and feelings on their children.
- Invite caregivers to consider how the impact of societal oppression on the caregivers may impact their children.
- Distinguish the child's external and internal worlds.
- Facilitator's may model imagining a child's experience to foster caregiver's sense of wondering.
- Look for in-the-moment ways to access intense affect.
- Begin where the caregiver is comfortable and emotionally regulated. If it is too overwhelming, there may be some delay on focusing on the caregiver-child dyad.

God Image Interventions

- Foster a contemplative space offering intentional reflective questions about God.
- Notice how caregivers feel toward God.
- Track caregivers' perceptions of how God may feel toward them.
- Invite new dialogues about hoped for experiences with God.
- Link parallels between caregivers' relationships with God and with their children.
- Link parallels between caregivers' relationships to society/religion and with their children.

In the following case example, I will share about a *Contemplative Focused Parenting* group I facilitated for caregivers of young children. Through validating experiences which have made it difficult for them to parent in preferred ways, we focus on their own attachment filters and begin to shift how they feel toward God and their perception of how God feels about them. This particular group was conducted in a low socioeconomic area, and various relevant sociocultural factors were included for reflection in the group sessions as a way to bring enhanced perspective beyond personal attributes as the primary rationale for caregiver sensitivity and ability to respond to their children. The groups continuously moved back and forth between infant observations, caregiver observations, and parallels among caregiver God images, experiences of societal oppression, and their relationship with their child.

Case Example: Facilitating a Parenting God Image Group

Jamie (pseudonym) is a 28-year-old African-American, Baptist Christian single mother of three children under the age of 5. Jamie was referred to the 8-week parenting group I led in a church near the domestic violence shelter, which was advertised as a parenting group focused on caregiver God images. Questions pertaining to client spiritual/religious coping, spiritual/religious beliefs, faith community engagement, and larger social context were included as part of the intake packet for the group (Esmiol Wilson, 2018). The following is an example of addressing ways in which societal inequity has challenged Jamie's preferred parenting, accessing Jamie's God image in order to bolster her attachment security with God, and promoting the development of her parental reflective functioning. In addition to the *Contemplative Focused Parenting* principles, aspects of the *justice-informed framework for spiritual and religious* resilience (Esmiol Wilson, 2018) will be applied in order to ethically empower Jamie in her preference to counter harmful aspects and incorporate more supportive aspects of her personal religious faith.

Addressing Social Inequity's Influence

Jamie resides in a low-income neighborhood in Los Angeles County and receives social services assistance with food and housing. At the time of treatment, she was unemployed and living in a domestic violence shelter after an emergency room visit due to a physical altercation with her boyfriend that resulted in a black eye. I directly asked her how she felt about being part of this group, and whether or not she had any concerns about me as a biracial woman and psychologist, about my perspectives, or my ability to connect with her experiences. She was thoughtful for a moment and then replied that she didn't want anyone to look down on her. I asked her about previous experiences of people looking down on her, which led to a rich discussion about the many ways (e.g., race, color of skin, gender, SES, education, employment, living situation, etc.) in which she'd been made to feel "less than." We talked about ways in which feelings of fear, insecurity, and being judged felt crippling to her and how it made it difficult for her to feel spiritually connected to God ("If God loves all of us equally, why is life so much more difficult for some than for others?") and to her daughter ("It's hard for me to think about what she needs when I'm so overwhelmed myself"). We also addressed ways in which she'd developed a strong sense of resilience at having overcome so many difficulties.

Jamie's Perception of How God Sees Her

Jamie attended the joint infant/caregiver parenting group with her 10-month-old daughter. From the first meeting, Jamie appeared to intermittently engage with her daughter while often seeming to be distracted. In group, we considered how God may feel and relate to the caregivers, and we reflected on similarities to the caregivers' feelings and responsiveness to their infants. During one of the first groups, I asked group members to imagine the face of God and then reflect on what feelings emerged for them. Jamie's initial response was that she imagined a loving God. She indicated, "I see God smiling at me. I see God's kindness and warmth in his eyes." As Jamie finished sharing with the group, she indicated the image she envisioned changed to a face filled with betrayal.

I asked Jamie what she thought prompted this shift in her God image. She said she wasn't sure, and I followed up with questions about other places where she'd experienced things not being as she'd anticipated or hoped. She talked about difficulties growing up and the confusion she felt seeing her parents treated differently because of the color of their skin. She talked about her own parenting and the fear she had for her baby growing up in a world that would likely be hurtful and unjust to her as well. All of these experiences were fraught with double messages, such as "You can be anything you want if you work hard enough," when that wasn't her reality, or "Looks don't matter," when clearly they did. It made sense then that her image of God was also complicated and that she feared that He might not see her as she needed Him to. At this point, I empathized with Jamie's experiences of inequality and being judged and inquired if others in the group had similar types of experiences. As other group members disclosed their backgrounds with societal oppression, Jamie's face appeared to soften toward a sense of openness to the group. I, then, welcomed group members to speak about their needs in a religious community for a sense of belonging and feeling valued (Esmiol Wilson, 2018). After a few of the others shared, Jamie disclosed the importance of acceptance and recognition of her experiences of racism and socioeconomic equity. Wanting to access some of Jamie's religious coping she described in her intake packet (e.g., prayer, journaling, seeking God for comfort during difficulties), I asked her, "What spiritually might feel helpful to you right now?" She paused and with what appeared to be a slight look of surprise, she expressed her desire to spend some time in prayer being honest with God about her feelings toward him and the impact of exclusion in society.

Jamie's Experience of God

As the group members and I attended to Jamie's own experiences of societal marginalization, I began to notice a shift in her ability to attune to her daughter's internal world. As she was cared for, she was in turn further able to pour energy into her daughter. Actions that at one time had seemed very personal ("when she throws a tantrum, she's just trying to upset me") now seemed less so, and Jamie was able to contextualize why her daughter might be responding that way. This mirrored our own process in the group of attending to why it had been challenging for so many of them to parent in their own preferred ways and how this made sense when taking into account experiences of marginalization and oppression that limited them. Jamie contributed to the group, "Since our last group, I've journaled and prayed being real with God. Maybe it helped you all listened and understood me, but it was nice because I felt God listened. I even had a sense of him being sad and just getting it. And when I thought about the guilt I feel not doing more for my daughter, it was like he got it and already knew." Jamie's new felt sense of God's compassion toward her and her experiences of oppression were warmly received by the other women.

Parallels Between Jamie's God Image and Her Relationship with Her Daughter

As Jamie felt understood and affirmed in her experiences, she continued to make shifts in attuning to her daughter in less reactive ways. However, she still felt "not enough" at times. As she shared this, she began to tear up. Wanting to access her in-the-moment affect and to reinforce positive religious coping, I explored how she imagined God understanding where she was coming from and, without judgment, responding to her in her sadness. She paused for a moment and then stated that while not her initial reaction, she was now able to picture God extending both comfort and a listening ear toward her. As she finished articulating her experience to the group, Jaime then extended her own hand toward her daughter and scooped her into her arms as her daughter began to whimper. Jaime expressed, "Sometimes, it helps for me to picture God being understanding and caring with me. That reminds me to be the same for her."

Final Thoughts

Viewing attachment not only through the lens of parents and infants, but also through individuals and larger society, can be helpful in understanding clients and supporting their preferred parenting approaches. The attachment style lays the blueprint for expectation in relationships with others and also provides the groundwork in relational expectation in the spiritual domain. It is critical for therapists to do continued self-reflection throughout this process so as not to impose ideas about parenting or God, but rather to expand on and support those aspects that are important to clients. As caregivers feel heard, understood, and validated in their own experiences (especially those of marginalization and injustice), they in turn may be able to better attune to their children and draw on a more supportive God image, which circularly may support their preferred parenting approach.

References

Ainsworth, M. D. S., Blehar, M. C., Waters, E., & Wall, S. (1978). *Patterns of attachment: A psychological study of the strange situation*. Hillsdale, NJ: Erlbaum.

Bowlby, J. (1982). *Attachment and loss: Vol. I. Attachment*. New York: Basic Books. (Original work published 1969).

Esmiol Wilson, E. (2018). From assessment to activism: Utilizing a justice-informed framework to guide spiritual and religious clinical interventions. In E. Esmiol Wilson & L. A. Nice (Eds.), *Socially just religious and spiritual interventions: Ethical uses of therapeutic power, AFTA Springer Briefs*. Cham, Switzerland: Springer.

Fonagy, P., & Target, M. (1998). Mentalization and the changing aims of child psychoanalysis. *Psychoanalytic Dialogues, 8*, 87–114.

Grimes, C. (2007). God image research: A literature review. In G. Moriarty & L. Hoffman (Eds.), *God image handbook for spiritual counseling and psychotherapy: Research, theory, and practice* (pp. 11–32). Binghamton, NY: Haworth Press.

Hays, P. A. (1996). Addressing the complexities of culture and gender in counseling. *Journal of Counseling and Development, 74*(4), 332–338.

Kirkpatrick, K. L. (1992). An attachment-theoretical approach to the psychology of religion. *International Journal for the Psychology of Religion, 2*, 3–38.

Lyons-Ruth, K., Bruschweiler-Stern, N., Harrison, A. M., Morgan, A. C., Nahum, J. P., Sander, L., et al. (1998). Implicit relational knowing: Its role in development and psychoanalytic treatment. *Infant Mental Health Journal, 19*, 282–289.

Main, M., & Solomon, J. (1990). Procedures for identifying infants as disorganized/disoriented during the Ainsworth strange situation. In M. T. Greenberg, D. Ciccheti, & E. M. Cummings (Eds.), *Attachment in the preschool years: Theory, research, and intervention* (pp. 121–160). Chicago: University of Chicago Press.

Nieto, L. (2010). *Beyond inclusion, beyond empowerment: A developmental strategy to liberate everyone*. Olympia, WA: Cuetzpalin.

Reynolds, D. (2003). Mindful parenting: A group approach to enhancing reflective capacity in parents and infants. *Journal of Child Psychology, 29*, 357–374.

Rizzuto, A. (1979). *The birth of the living God*. Chicago: University of Chicago Press.

Slade, A. (2005). Parental reflective functioning: An introduction. *Attachment & Human Development, 7*, 269–281.

Slade, A. (2006). Reflective parenting programs: Theory and development. *Psychoanalytic Inquiry, 26*, 640–657.

Thomas, M. J., Moriarty, G. L., Davis, E. B., & Anderson, E. L. (2011). The effects of a manualized group-psychotherapy intervention on client God images and attachment to God: A pilot study. *Journal of Psychology and Theology, 39*, 44–58.

Wallin, D. J. (2007). *Attachment in psychotherapy*. New York: The Guilford Press.

Chapter 11
Making Each Moment Count: Supporting Justice-Informed, Whole-Person Health in Hospital-Based Brief Therapy for Acute Illness

Lindsey Nice

A significant amount of research connects spiritual health to whole-person health, healing, and well-being (Engel, 1980; Wright, Watson, & Bell, 1996). As a family systems therapist, I value systems theory, which tells me that all intersecting aspects of our identities are important. As a medical family therapist (MedFT), I work from a BioPsychoSocial-Spiritual (BPSS) model, where inclusion of all parts helps foster better outcomes. However, many family therapists and MedFTs are hesitant to integrate spirituality into their care (Harris, Randolph, & Gordon, 2016). In circumstances where time is of the essence, for example, with patients and families experiencing acute illness, drawing on patient spirituality may be a powerful resource. In this chapter, I explore the relationship between faith and acute illness and the clinical implications of addressing religion and spirituality in hospital-based brief therapy, with two examples from my own clinical work.

Spirituality has been a part of my own life for as long as I can remember. I am a third-generation Seventh-day Adventist and consider this faith community the primary part of my identity. In most ways, this provides the foundation for my social justice work as a family therapist. I've learned that I can hold on to the parts of my religion that are central to who I am: faith practices that sustain me and support me becoming a better, more compassionate person while also rejecting and actively working against constraining elements that are harmful to myself and others. I continue to be thankful for those friends and colleagues in similar and different spiritual paths who continue to walk with me on the journey.

Medical family therapy has been a significant part of my professional life as well. I chose to go into this specialty because of a medical crisis in my own family and changed careers from nursing to family therapy. While completing my PhD in California, I spent 2 years working at an 800-bed, Level 1 trauma center as a medical

L. Nice (✉)
Marriage and Family Therapy Program, Pacific Lutheran University, Tacoma, WA, USA
e-mail: lawsonla@plu.edu

E. Esmiol Wilson, L. Nice (eds.), *Socially Just Religious and Spiritual Interventions*, AFTA SpringerBriefs in Family Therapy, https://doi.org/10.1007/978-3-030-01986-0_11

family therapist, seeing patients and families who were typically experiencing some kind of healthcare crisis, rather than a long-term chronic illness. My approach to MedFT is shaped by this experience, and in this chapter, I will describe integrating spirituality into medical family therapy when time may be limited and illness is acute. In addition, I will use the term "patient," rather than "client," as this is consistent with the language of medical contexts.

Guiding Theories and Definitions

Religion and Spirituality

"Religion" and "spirituality" are often used interchangeably but mean different things. Hill and Pargament (2003) describe religion as being an "organized faith system" and a specific culture that may include common traditions, beliefs, values, and practices. Prest, Russel, and D'Souza (1999) describe spirituality as a broader concept that incorporates the common human experience of finding meaning, purpose, and fulfillment in life. Religion and spirituality intersect with other parts of our identities: most of us occupy both privileged and marginalized positions, and these levels intersect in complicated ways (Crenshaw, 1991). Similarly, religion and spirituality can be used in ways that are helpful and ways that are harmful. For the purpose of this chapter, I will focus on how to support those helpful aspects of religion and spirituality that encourage whole-person health and counter harmful aspects that may limit healing.

Relevance of Spirituality to Patients

Even though spirituality is an important part of whole-person health, it is the least attended to piece of the BPSS model (Delbridge, Taylor, & Hanson, 2014). This is a critical problem for many reasons. Issues that bring clients to therapy in general are often tied to religious or spiritual beliefs (Richards & Bergin, 2000), and for many coping with medical issues, spirituality, and its search for meaning seem to go hand in hand. Some see medical issues as the result of spiritual failings on their part or as part of a bigger plan (Koenig, Moberg, & Kvale, 1988), while others see spirituality as a helpful support in times of crisis (Pargament, 1997). While it's clear that spirituality and religion are important components of many peoples' lives, not only MedFT patients' faith but psychotherapy clients' faiths are often missed in therapy completely or even pathologized by therapists (Esmiol Wilson, 2018).

Link Between Spiritual Health and Physical and Mental Well-Being

Spiritual health has been shown to have concrete effects on physical well-being for a variety of illnesses (Hill & Pargament, 2003) and for highly marginalized populations such as LGBTQ individuals (Hughes, Damin, & Heiden-Rootes, 2017), low-income families (Pandit, 2013), and Latinx (Willerton, Dankoski, & Martir, 2008), to name a few. Spiritual well-being while coping with illness has also been linked to improved mental health, including increased levels of hope and decreased anxiety and depression (Lin & Bauer-Wu, 2003).

Clinician's Role

In any type of therapy, the relationship we form with patients is our foundation for effective work (Sprenkle, Davis, & Lebow, 2013). A relationship where clients feel heard, understood, and respected becomes vitally important when we address issues of spirituality, which often touches on the most vulnerable parts of ourselves. I see three key places for intervention when working with acute illness patients around issues of spirituality:

1. IDENTIFY how faith is impacting the patient/family.
2. INTERRUPT ways that faith is undermining healing and whole-person health.
3. REINFORCE new, supportive, and expanded definitions of faith.

In the following two case studies, I will demonstrate applying medical family therapy with special attention to the larger social context and will describe ways to use the three-step intervention above to help patients and families in acute medical crisis draw on religion and spirituality as supportive sources of healing.

Case Study #1

I was asked by the psychiatry team to work with a client who had initially been referred to them because of the assumed possibility of psychosomatic illness. The man had been struck by what he described as "paralyzing pain" while doing the dishes at his sink a week prior. The medical team had run a battery of tests trying to figure out the cause of this pain, with dead ends at every turn. Unable to discharge him in his current state, they turned to psychiatry to find out if this was in fact a mental rather than physical problem.

Biological Aspects

This patient – I will call him Binh – was Vietnamese-American in his late 70s. He was in physically good shape, although he appeared somewhat frail and pallid after being in the hospital for almost a week. I asked if he'd noticed any changes prior to the aggravating incident in his physical health or if he had any idea what had caused this "shooting pain." He replied "I don't know," to most of my questions and seemed uninterested in talking with me.

Psychological Aspects

When I walked into the room, Binh was facing the other direction, curled in the hospital bed with the sheets pulled up around his shoulders. I remember him being tearful at times and emotionless at others. I became concerned about him being depressed but still wasn't able to make any links between his psychological state and the physical pain he was experiencing.

Social Aspects

While I tried several times to reach out to his wife and daughters, I wasn't able to connect with them while Binh was hospitalized. This was an especially challenging aspect of our work, as I served as an "on call" therapist who would go from room to room as needed and wasn't always available to accommodate quick changes of plans when family members would arrive.

Spiritual Aspects

I was able to see Binh for about 30 min for each of 3 days in a row but felt like we weren't making progress. I kept wondering if there was something else I hadn't discovered – something that perhaps he didn't trust me to know yet. It wasn't until the third and final visit that I asked about his spiritual life. He described his conversion to Christianity and the importance that held for him. I noticed that he described a very "rigid" relationship with God, where if he should make a mistake, he worried God would punish him or fail to forgive him. I asked if this was similar to or different than his relationship with other important figures in his life, and he responded that he connected to his father in a similar way. At the same time, I was internally reflecting on my own values around faith and how my bias toward a less-hierarchical relationship with God was likely a reflection of my own Western, Eurocentric values.

Finally, I asked if or how Binh's relationship with God was impacting him now. I noticed a distinct shift in his posture: he paused and quietly thought for a few moments before telling me that the day he was standing in front of his sink doing dishes, he'd been frustrated with multiple aspects of his life, and the thought passed through his mind that he should turn his back on God. He recalled how immediately after this, he felt the searing pain in his back that brought him into the hospital. With tears running down his face, he described how he was certain that God had turned His back on him because he'd committed "the unpardonable sin" of denying God and "turning my back on the Holy Spirit."

Greater Social Context

I also needed to consider Binh in the greater social context. He'd moved to the USA as a first-generation immigrant in the 1980s and settled in Southern California with his wife and two daughters. English was not his first language, and I knew he struggled when the medical teams stood around his bed, often in a hurry, and asked him question after question. I asked about the cultural aspects from Vietnam that continued to be important to him, and he talked about kinship and the value of the collective whole over any one person's own individual needs. I asked what it was like for him to be here – in a place where the focus was solely on him – and where he didn't have many choices. He replied that it was difficult.

Interventions

I felt early on in my time with Binh that there was a missing piece – something that wasn't safe for him to disclose to me until he felt comfortable – that would connect his presenting symptoms to something identifiable. When he disclosed to me his fear that he'd committed the unpardonable sin – turning his back on the Holy Spirit – the intersecting pieces of his experience made sense (IDENTIFYING). Coming from a culture that closely connected physical health and spiritual health, the physical pain he felt made sense as a somatic manifestation of his spiritual distress. Hearing that he didn't trust that anyone would believe him or take him seriously also made sense considering the cultural clash and context of Western medicine.

I was worried that this view of God wouldn't be helpful for his healing, but I didn't know how to challenge it in a contextually respectful way. It wouldn't have worked, or been consistent with his social context, to push a Western individualist view of Christianity on him. I wanted to challenge and expand his rigid definition of his relationship with God, but I had to do that in a way that stayed true to his value around kinship. I decided to focus on the relationship he'd talked about as being especially helpful to him: his wife. We reflected on what particularly it was about her that created such a feeling of trust and care between them, and he said that it "felt like she could see his heart."

This felt like a potentially healing piece to me, and I cautiously connected this back to the earlier conversation we had about God (INTERRUPT). I inquired about times when he'd felt like God could see his heart and whether or not there was possibility that his relationship with God, like that of his wife, could accommodate mistakes. We finished the remainder of our time together reflecting on this possibility that God could see his heart and that perhaps He could understand mistakes in the same relational, kinship-oriented way his wife had so many times over the years (REINFORCE).

Case Study #2

I was asked to work with a young African-American Muslim couple who recently experienced severe post-birth complications, including a significant kidney infection. The female partner had been hospitalized for about a week before I was referred to them and was in a controlled infection unit where all visitors had to "gown up" before going through several sets of doors into her room. Her baby was being held in the neonatal intensive care unit (NICU), and she hadn't seen her in several days. I was able to see this couple for an unusual amount of time: daily for a week. Our visits varied according to the needs of the day: some days I spent an hour with them and others only a few minutes.

Biological Aspects

I'll call the female partner Layla and the male partner Jordan. Layla was a young mother – in her early 20s – and this was her first pregnancy. Together with Jordan, she'd hoped and dreamed about what parenthood would be like, none of which included prolonged hospitalization. Layla's kidney infection was the extension of a bladder infection caused by catheterization during birth. The infection had gone undetected for several days but then flared up to where her medical team was now concerned about sepsis – a condition where the body's response to infection in one area causes inflammation throughout the rest of the body and can result in organ shutdown. Layla was on heavy doses of antibiotics to help reduce this risk and was being carefully monitored day and night.

Psychological Aspects

Layla was extremely tearful and distressed; most days when I arrived, she immediately burst into tears. I remember her keeping a photo of the baby at the foot of her bed so that she could "see" her often, even with the distance between them. I worried about Layla facing depression and relational problems as a result of the stress this was causing. Jordan was much more stoic and seemed hesitant to engage with me.

Social Aspects

Jordan and Layla had a close African-American community of support around them. They were very connected to family in the area and had a near-constant stream of people dropping off cards and flowers in the lobby. This seemed to be an incredible support to both of them.

Spiritual Aspects

In our first few days together, I asked Layla and Jordan about their spiritual lives and what gave them meaning. Layla replied that they were both Muslim and that they felt a strong sense of direction and purpose in loving and serving Allah. I inquired about the history of their faith and the ways this had supported and sustained them through difficult times, and Layla replied that she was having a difficult time feeling Allah's presence with them now. It seemed significant that she described this in a relational way: as collective and not just her individual experience. She felt "punished" by Allah and wondered why He would allow something like this to happen to them. I asked Jordan if he shared a similar feeling, and he responded that they needed to "keep faith" and was concerned that her doubt was a reflection of spiritual weakness.

Greater Social Context

My supervisor would join me every week for several sessions and would do co-therapy with me. She joined on this particular case and reflected to me afterward that I didn't seem myself with this couple. She wondered why that was and asked if I had talked with them about our own contextual difference of race. I replied that I hadn't and agreed with her that this was likely impacting our work together. In the next session, I directly addressed this by asking the couple what it was like to work with me – one part of their mostly White care team. There were visible signs of relief when I asked this question, and the couple opened up to me in new ways. They acknowledged wondering if I had any life experiences that would assist me in understanding their own; I reflected appreciation for their transparency and asked what they were most concerned about me understanding. They reflected on their mostly White medical care team, feelings of inferiority in the face of their "expertise," and initially seeing me as another part of that team.

Interventions

When Jordan reflected on Layla's spiritual struggles as "weakness," I asked if or how spirituality and race together had impacted their lives. Jordan talked about how the meaning of "giving up" or "doubting" meant to him something very different than it meant to me – it reflected weakness that could cost him his life (IDENTIFY). I understood better that it was incredibly frightening for him to hear his wife talk this way and that it triggered his own fears – many of them shaped by the systemic racism he'd experienced – about uncertainty, abandonment, etc. Hearing Jordan share his fears impacted Layla in a totally different way than the previous conversation. Once she experienced her doubts as triggering intense fear for him rather than him seeing her doubts as a personal failing of her own, she could soften and empathize with him (INTERRUPT). Together we framed both of their fears as a common thread between them, one that could be appreciated as a sign of their ability to be truly authentic and vulnerable with one another and together turn to Allah for support (REINFORCE). While Layla's medical complications continued for several weeks, she reported increased levels of hope and decreased symptoms of depression until she and Jordan were discharged home with their daughter.

Clinical Implications

These two case studies demonstrate the importance of clients' spiritual needs in acute medical situations and the need for MedFTs to attend to spiritual issues. I will frame clinical implications around the two primary goals of medical family therapy: increasing patients' sense of AGENCY, or ability to take part in decision-making and have access to options that are right for them, and increasing their sense of COMMUNION, or safety, secure attachment, and connection to others around them (McDaniel, Hepworth, & Doherty, 1992).

Increasing Patient Agency

Creating Space Through Inviting Spiritual Self-Reflection The responsibility of creating space for conversations about the intersecting pieces of our identities – race, gender, religion, etc. – falls to us as therapists. Patients may feel hesitant to bring up concerns around spirituality if we fail to ask about them. This often requires a good deal of our own self-work. The very process of reflecting on what is helpful or harmful about faith practices is not neutral! This should be done with constant care and self-reflection so as not to colonize. Therapists who are unfamiliar or uncomfortable discussing aspects of spirituality may need to seek out necessary resources and support to increase confidence (Walsh, 2008). This need is only intensified in hospital-based brief therapy where one may have days not of weeks to inquire about faith.

In teaching first-year MFT students, I ask them to reflect on how their own spiritual and religious orientation might impact their work with a therapist if they were the clients. For example, as an atheist or agnostic, what fears or concerns might you have in working with a religious therapist? What assumptions might they make about you? How does this belief system ground your worldview? How does it impact your relationships with others? What might you need if you were working with someone from a different perspective, i.e., someone who is quite religious? For many, doing this self-reflection enables therapists to create more direct space for conversations around spirituality in therapy.

Spiritual Assessment Understanding what meaning patients ascribe to their illness is often closely linked to spirituality and may help MedFTs know where best to intervene. Providers should be prepared to include spiritual assessment as part of their care plan. This can take many forms, including questions such as "does your illness have meaning for you?" "Does it allow you to be more aware of yourself, to relate differently to people, family, nature, or to the meaningfulness of your being and actions?" (Ben-Ayre, Steinmetz, & Ezzo, 2007). Therapists may use tools such as a spiritual genogram (Frame, 2000) or can help patients create an illness narrative (Charon, 2006). Assessment measures such as the spiritual well-being scale (Ellison, 1983) or spiritual assessment inventory (Hall & Edwards, 1996) can guide conversation as well. Choosing one of these assessment tools and becoming familiar with spiritually-oriented questions are essential in brief therapy as hospital-based MedFTs may not treat patients long enough to administer multiple assessments.

Increasing Patient Communion

Attending to Spiritual Connections In the limited time frame of most medical family therapy interventions, attending to patients' pre-established spiritual connections may help to quickly foster a sense of safety, secure attachment, and connection to the therapist. Therapists can model specific skills, including attunement and empathy when inquiring about patients' faith backgrounds, direct communication when addressing helpful and harmful aspects of spirituality, and embracing vulnerability with clients who are facing medical crises or uncertainty in the future. All of these interventions should be framed through the lens of respectful, patient-centered care.

Relational Spirituality We know that illness impacts more than just the patient and that family members often feel the effects as strongly as their loved ones coping with medical issues. A "relationally spiritual" approach may have a positive impact on couple and family relationships as people face illness together (Mahoney, 2010). Helping couples and families establish mutually supportive relationships with each other may also have a positive impact on their spiritual lives, as they begin to mirror patterns of intimacy rather than obligation, even in the face of significant challenges (Esmiol Wilson, Knudson-Martin, & Wilson, 2014). Therefore, assessing for and working with spirituality as a core component of relational care may have benefits that go beyond just the individual patient to impact whole-family health.

Linking to the Larger Medical Context Medical family therapists are often the "bridge" between patients and their medical providers. While chaplains may primarily support patients' spiritual lives, and medical providers their physical needs, MedFTs may be the connection between these. Historically healthcare providers, and especially physicians, have been hesitant to include patients' spiritual concerns in medical treatment (Anandarajah & Hight, 2001); however, increased support from MedFTs may be helpful in integrating spiritual issues as part of standard care. Healthcare providers who learn to shift from their role of "educator" to "curious listener" will do this well (Hodgson, Lamson, Mendenhall, & Crane, 2014).

References

Anandarajah, G., & Hight, E. (2001). Spirituality and medical practice: Using the HOPE questions as a practical tool for spiritual assessment. *American Family Physician, 63*, 81–88.

Ben-Ayre, E., Steinmetz, D., & Ezzo, J. (2007). Two women and cancer: The need for addressing spiritual well-being in cancer care. *Families, Systems & Health, 25*(1), 1–9.

Charon, R. (2006). *Narrative medicine: Stories that heal*. New York: Oxford University Press.

Crenshaw, K. (1991). Mapping the margins: Intersectionality, identity politics, and violence against women of color. *Stanford Law Review, 43*(6), 1241–1299.

Delbridge, E., Taylor, J., & Hanson, C. (2014). Honoring the "spiritual" in biopsychosocial-spiritual health care: Medical family therapists on the front lines of graduate education, clinical practice, and research. In J. Hodgson, A. Lamson, T. Mendenhall, & R. Crane (Eds.), *Medical family therapy* (pp. 196–218). Cham, Switzerland: Springer International Publishing.

Ellison, C. W. (1983). Spiritual well-being: Conceptualization and measurement. *Journal of Psychology and Theology, 11*(4), 330–340.

Engel, G. L. (1980). The clinical application of the biopsychosocial model. *American Journal of Psychiatry, 137*, 535–544.

Esmiol Wilson, E. (2018). From assessment to activism: Utilizing a justice-informed framework to guide spiritual and religious clinical interventions. In E. Esmiol Wilson & L. A. Nice (Eds.), *Socially just religious and spiritual interventions: Ethical uses of therapeutic power, AFTA Springer Briefs*. Cham, Switzerland: Springer.

Esmiol Wilson, E., Knudson-Martin, C., & Wilson, C. (2014). Gendered power, spirituality, and relational processes: Experiences of Christian physician couples. *Journal of Couple and Relationship Therapy, 13*(4), 312–338.

Frame, M. (2000). The spiritual genogram in family therapy. *Journal of Marital and Family Therapy, 26*(2), 211–216.

Hall, T. W., & Edwards, K. J. (1996). The initial development and factor analysis of the spiritual assessment inventory. *Journal of Psychology and Theology, 24*(3), 233–246.

Harris, K., Randolph, B., & Gordon, T. (2016). What do clients want? Assessing spiritual needs in counseling: A literature review. *Spirituality in Clinical Practice, 3*(4), 250–275.

Hill, P. C., & Pargament, K. I. (2003). Advanced in the conceptualization and measurement of religion and spirituality. *American Psychologist, 58*(1), 64–74.

Hodgson, J., Lamson, A., Mendenhall, T., & Crane, D. R. (2014). *Medical family therapy: Advanced applications*. Cham, Switzerland: Springer International Publishing.
Hughes, R., Damin, C., & Heiden-Rootes, K. (2017). Where's the LGBT in integrated care research? A systemic review. *Families, Systems & Health, 35*, 308–319. Online first publication: August 14, 2017.
Koenig, H. G., Moberg, D. O., & Kvale, J. N. (1988). Religious activities of older adults in a geriatric assessment clinic. *Journal of American Geriatrics Society, 36*, 362–374.
Lin, H. R., & Bauer-Wu, S. M. (2003). Psycho- spiritual well-being in patients with advanced cancer: An integrative review of the literature. *Journal of Advanced Nursing, 44*, 69–80.
Mahoney, A. (2010). Religion in families, 1999–2009: A relational spirituality framework. *Journal of Marriage and Family, 72*, 805–827.
McDaniel, S. H., Hepworth, J., & Doherty, W. J. (Eds.). (1992). *Medical family therapy: A biopsychosocial approach to families with health problems*. New York: Basic Books.
Pandit, M. (2013). *Study of brief single session medical family therapy with low-income patients* (Unpublished doctoral dissertation). Loma Linda University, Loma Linda, CA.
Pargament, K. I. (1997). *The psychology of religion and coping: Theory, research, and practice*. New York: The Guilford Press.
Prest, L. A., Russel, R., & D'Souza, H. (1999). Spirituality and religion in training, practice, and personal development. *Journal of Family Therapy, 21*, 60–77.
Richards, P. S., & Bergin, A. E. (Eds.). (2000). *Handbook of psychotherapy and religious diversity*. Washington, DC: American Psychological Association New York: The Guilford Press.
Sprenkle, D., Davis, S., & Lebow, J. (2013). *Common factors in couple and family therapy: The overlooked foundation for effective practice*. New York: The Guilford Press.
Walsh, F. (2008). Religion, spirituality and the family: Multifaith perspectives. In F. Walsh (Ed.), *Spiritual resources in family therapy* (pp. 3–30). New York: Guilford Press.
Willerton, E., Dankoski, M. E., & Sevilla Martir, J. F. (2008). Medical family therapy: A model for addressing mental health disparities among Latinos. *Families, Systems & Health, 26*, 196–206.
Wright, L. M., Watson, W. L., & Bell, J. M. (1996). *Beliefs: The heart of healing in families and illness*. New York: Basic Books.

Chapter 12
Supporting Whole-Person Health: Socially Just Application of Religion and Spirituality in an Outpatient Care Facility for Individuals with Chronic Illnesses

Sarah K. Samman

Despite the universality of illness, individuals and their families often experience a sense of fear, isolation, and vulnerability as they are confronted with the finite and fragile reality of the human condition. An illness diagnosis can directly and negatively impact individuals, families, support persons/systems, and society and commonly results in marked shifts in roles and relational patterns between members of the system (McDaniel, Doherty, & Hepworth, 2014; McDaniel, Hepworth, & Doherty, 1992). Illness experiences, particularly those related to chronic illnesses, can invite existential questions and struggles that are perhaps being considered for the first time within the self and in relation to others. As such, social experiences and influences are an integral part of the illness experience (Engel, 1977) and often include spiritual and religious components. Thus, integrating spirituality and religion, i.e., the Sacred, into illness narratives allows for a more expansive evaluation of the human experience.

In this chapter I will highlight the importance of medical family therapists (MedFTs) attending to the wholeness of the systemic experience using BioPsychoSocial-Spiritual (BPSS) interventions reflected in a case example of a couple diagnosed with end-stage renal disease. I then briefly provide a demonstration of how to assess for empowering and oppressive experiences with the Sacred and conclude with a summary of clinical recommendations.

S. K. Samman (✉)
Couple and Family Therapy Program, Alliant University, San Diego campus, San Diego, CA, USA
e-mail: sarah.samman@alliant.edu

E. Esmiol Wilson, L. Nice (eds.), *Socially Just Religious and Spiritual Interventions*, AFTA SpringerBriefs in Family Therapy, https://doi.org/10.1007/978-3-030-01986-0_12

Medical Family Therapy

The long-standing divide between the biological focus of medical care and the psychological and social components of mental healthcare has shifted as evidenced by the emergence of medical family therapy (MedFT; McDaniel et al., 1992). MedFT is a subspecialty of marriage and family therapy with the overarching goal to promote *agency*, i.e., the ability of clients and families to advocate for self, and *communion*, i.e., the ability to develop and maintain bonds (McDaniel et al., 2014) with family, the healthcare system, and the Sacred (Hodgson, Lamson, & Reese, 2007).

MedFTs and the Inclusion of the Sacred

As the field of MedFT evolved, Hodgson et al. (2007) recommended the explicit addition of spirituality to the biopsychosocial interview (see also Esmiol Wilson, 2018). The Sacred often has positive influences, helps to identify solutions and resources, makes meaning, motivates change, and influences relationships (Aponte, 2002). More specifically, Ramirez et al. (2012) found religious coping associated with improved health-related quality of life (QOL) in their population. Conversely, Ramirez et al. found that religious struggle was associated with depression, anxiety, and decreased health-related QOL (see also Aponte, 2002). Thus, incorporating the Sacred when expanding agency and communion allows MedFTs to identify and harness the benefits of the Sacred while countering and mitigating the harm.

Challenges Discussing the Sacred

It can be difficult to make sense of the Sacred, let alone share or explain these experiences to others. Therapists can further exacerbate challenges with the Sacred when they fail to consider the impact of their own beliefs and assumptions and may rely on a reductionist approach to cultural competence (Hoogestraat & Trammel). Thus, therapists must understand the values, biases, and limitations of – and often suspend – their own Sacred worldview to respectfully explore and intervene compatibly with clients and their families' worldviews, goals, and resources.

Author's Location of Self

I identify as a heterosexual, cisgender, white, Arab and European-American, dual citizen, middle-class, formally educated, able-bodied, Muslim woman, spouse, mother, friend, teacher, supervisor, and mentor. I am also fluent in English and several dialects of Arabic, which allows me to recognize the nuanced ways in which language affects individuals and families. I view myself as an intersectional feminist actively resisting oppressive discourses and committed to equality and justice both personally and clinically. This includes respecting, exploring, and harnessing empowering stories of the Sacred.

I previously worked in a co-located, secondary care, outpatient facility supporting individuals with chronic illnesses and their families. I commonly presented in a one-down position to establish myself as a healthcare team member while simultaneously highlighting my evaluative and clinical value to the team. I worked with patients of different ages, ethnicities, citizenships, and residency statuses with liver, kidney, and heart disease. I identify as a social constructionist and believe society and individuals, particularly those struggling with chronic illnesses within the healthcare system, and are continually constructing realities within larger systems of inequality, particularly around social locations such as gender as well as residency and socioeconomic status. Therefore, my approach to the Sacred is largely focused on assessing for the harmful or helpful influences of the Sacred on individuals and the system as a whole, using therapeutic power to explore and co-create empowering Sacred experiences while deconstructing those that are oppressive (see Esmiol Wilson, 2018).

Case Example: Supporting the Whole System Through End-Stage Renal Disease

Cindy, a 58-year-old female, presented to couple therapy with her 64-year-old spouse, Robert, due to recent psychosocial concerns impacting her eligibility for kidney transplantation listing (case details were modified, and pseudonyms were used to protect the confidentiality of the clients). The heterosexual couple had been married for 41 years and identified as Native American elders from a tribe in Southern California. Cindy was diagnosed with chronic kidney disease (CKD) at the age of 51 and was promptly placed on dialysis for 3 h a day, three times a week. She was also diagnosed with diabetes and heart disease as she experienced progressive kidney failure leading to a recent diagnosis of end-stage renal disease (ESRD). The couple decided to pursue transplantation listing. Robert identified as her primary caregiver and suffered from a list of medical conditions including liver disease, minor cognitive impairment, chronic fatigue, and insomnia in large part due to his history of alcohol abuse. He reported commitment and success with sobriety since Cindy was diagnosed with CKD.

Couple's Social Locations

Prior to the diagnosis of CKD, Cindy worked as a nurse practitioner and Robert was a contractor. Although both retired, they continued to work within their community, Cindy as an elder teaching their native language and spiritual beliefs and Robert increasing awareness of social injustice toward Native Americans. They described their current income as "barely covering living expenses and medical bills." The couple had one adult male child, Mathew, currently living in another state and minimally involved in their illness experiences. They also had two adult children who died traumatic deaths, one to gun violence 6 years prior and the other due to a drug overdose 4 years earlier.

Couple's Relationship with the Sacred

The couple reported dealing with the deaths of their children in significantly different ways. Cindy relied on her Sacred orientation, while Robert distanced himself from their "spiritual roots" due to overwhelming "despair." During a private meeting with her social worker, Cindy shared that her illness experience is worsening and believed a "spiritual reawakening" and community involvement would positively impact her individual health outcomes and their overall well-being.

MedFTs' Case Conceptualization of ESRD

Individuals with ESRD commonly suffer from the progressive decrease and eventual permanent loss of kidney functioning (Pruchno, Wilson-Genderson, & Cartwright, 2009; Timmers et al., 2008) and are commonly placed on dialysis. They frequently experience chronic fatigue, itching, dialysis pain, and sleep complaints (Pruchno et al., 2009; Ramirez et al., 2012; Timmers et al.., 2008; Yong et al., 2009). Psychological and relational changes may include increased stress/distress, depression, anxiety, and guilt; decreased self-esteem, coping, and marital satisfaction; impaired QOL; and general decline in physical and mental health with a greater frequency of suicide (Pruchno et al., 2009; Ramirez et al., 2012; Timmers et al., 2008; Yong et al., 2009).

As the MedFT assigned to the case, I was responsible for therapy services for the couple, consultation with other healthcare team members, advocacy, and mentoring through the process of awaiting transplantation. As part of my work, I assessed for illness-related beliefs, support system, and coping strategies through the application of agency and communion, illness and personal identification, and future orientation, ending with a final summary report of recommendations for or against kidney transplant listing.

Interventions to Include the Sacred

Assess for the Sacred As the couple shared struggles processing the traumatic loss of their two adult children, I assessed for agency and communion to help facilitate their grief. I inquired about general resources, their social support network, faith community, and individual and shared level of Sacred beliefs and practices (see Hodge, 2005; Hoogestraat & Trammel, 2003) that influence their illness experiences and sense of agency and communion. The following conversation was from our third couple session:

Therapist: As each of you shared your stories and experiences with illness, I couldn't help but hear several references to spiritual or religious beliefs and values. How would you describe your views as spiritual or religious beings?
Robert: Religious? Not anymore. I turned to my spiritual roots in my teens. It felt like the right thing at the time. But that's changed somewhat. It just kind of happened.
Therapist: What does that mean, to "turn to your spiritual roots"?
Robert: I still identify as Christian. But as a Native, I felt it lacked the connection and devotion to the Earth. So as a teen, I sought out my elders and reconnected with our land. Fasted, prayed, chanted. Tough physical stuff. I took part in the Sundance Ceremonies [Robert smiles]. The first time [Robert grimaces], it was the most painful thing I'd experienced in my life but nothing like giving birth [he holds Cindy's hand].
Therapist: That's a spiritually significant ceremony. What was the experience like for you? You mentioned some of the physical already [laughs], I mean in other ways?
Cindy: It's really hard to watch but when you think of the meaning behind the ritual, it's powerful to witness. But he hasn't been active as a spiritual elder in a long while.
Robert: It's not a bad thing. It's because I don't want to get any infections and get sicker and I'm taking you to and from your appointments. Those are my priorities now.
Cindy: You know that's not it. You haven't been the same the last few years. You're not as active and you don't even go to Church. You avoid talking about it altogether.
Robert: Cindy, it's not a big deal. My spirituality is in my heart now not my actions.
Cindy: For you. But I need to do more. I need something to help me get through the day-to-day. When things get rough, I need something stronger to depend on.
Therapist: Cindy, I hear you'd like Robert to be as spiritually active as before, though it seems he feels pretty comfortable where he is right now. And it sounds like his involvement would help you deal with your struggles... maybe provide you with spiritual strength? In what ways would spirituality help you cope with your illness experiences?
Cindy: I wake up in pain every day. I'm tired and achy and I've found that rituals help me a lot, especially tolerating procedures. But it's hard to feel motivated when you're in that painful place. I go to Church. I ask for help, but don't always get it the way I want.
Robert: But you've told me you've been relying on your friends for support and going to Church. You told me you're doing fine and I believed you.
Therapist: Cindy, you've shared you're not feeling like you're getting your spiritual needs met and you'd like that to change. Robert, what if you learned she isn't as able to meet her spiritual needs the way they are now? What would you say or do?
Robert: I guess I could ask her.
Therapist: You could. It sounds like she's told you she's struggling to manage her illness and concerned about spiritually connecting with you. That she feels you're not on the same page. And it seems like you have been feeling ambivalent about reigniting your spiritual connections. What would be different about how you ask her this time?
Robert: I don't know what to ask. I don't know where to start.
Therapist: Seems like you'd like to start somewhere. Does that mean you may be contemplating doing something differently, maybe to support your illness experiences?

In the above, I acknowledged and affirmed their individual illness experiences and those connected to the Sacred while highlighting Cindy's desire for greater Sacred connection with Robert and their community. I also accepted Robert's unreciprocated responses. I predominantly used open-ended questions to assess for level of interest or ambivalence about re-engaging with Sacred experiences without imposing an agenda and with awareness of my potential biases as a person of faith.

I recognized Cindy's agency and strong desire to connect throughout the session, while Robert appeared initially ambivalent and then open to considering a change in level of communion.

Explore Empowering and Oppressive Experiences with the Sacred Although the couple disagreed about why Robert's connection to the Sacred had changed, he appeared to generate agency and communion in support of Cindy and her needs. Later in the session, I explored both empowering and oppressive Sacred beliefs and behaviors:

> **Therapist:** I'm a little curious based on what you've shared so far if you could speak to how you consider your Sacred beliefs to be a personal or shared strength or limitation?
> **Robert:** What do you mean?
> **Therapist:** I've heard about your upbringing, your choice to pursue a Sacred avenue in your teens, to be involved in Sacred rituals, to be a spiritual elder. How do your beliefs and behaviors affect you? Could you speak to how you find them helpful or harmful?
> **Robert:** Well, even though I identify as Christian, I'm also a Native. I'm not naïve. I know how religion was used to oppress my people and how we were stripped of our lives, values, and heritage. It's easier for me to feel physically and emotionally tired, overwhelmed, and pull away. I see how that affects Cindy and her symptoms. I'm tired and don't have the spiritual fight in me anymore when I'm focused on our daily needs.
> **Cindy:** Honey, I'm so sorry. I knew you've always struggled with interpretations of the Church, but I couldn't understand why you gave up on the elders, on our community.
> **Therapist:** It sounds like you both have been going through a lot of physical and emotional changes lately and it seemed easier for Robert to manage by pulling away from his experiences with the Sacred. Robert, you had mentioned you are spiritual in your heart but not in actions. How does the Sacred encourage you to handle these adversities?
> **Robert:** I believe my elders taught me to turn to the Earth for answers. Like with my alcoholism, I wasn't honoring the Earth, my relationship with my surroundings, family, and community. I've been busy distracting myself from losing my children. I wasn't present and I was resentful. I lost my way. Which is why I'm happy I got a wakeup call and had to decide to get sober or lose Cindy. I'm not connected to the community like I was, but I'm in recovery now and things could look different maybe in the future.
> **Therapist:** Sounds like you may be considering reconnecting to the community. How could that be helpful managing your illness experience and supporting her in hers?
> **Robert:** Well, I know I'm not ready to reconnect to the Church just yet. It's not that I've lost faith in God. Connecting to the community would help awaken my sense of connection and passion to give back. I've enjoyed helping the new generations develop their Native identities. I think that's something that can give me focus and purpose again.
> **Therapist:** It sounds like you have an interest brewing. Cindy, I haven't heard from you in a while. What are your thoughts, and what do you appreciate about your Sacred beliefs?
> **Cindy:** It's good to hear him talk about his passions again. I see that glimmer in his eyes and it warms my heart. I don't doubt God because of what others did in His name. I personally haven't had issues consolidating Christian interpretations, so I guess that's a strength. I think they go hand in hand and see both of them supporting my illness experiences. I just know that I'd be happier to share the journey with Robert and others.

As Robert discussed painful experiences with the Christian Church, I noticed how they influenced his decision to disconnect from both Sacred communities in ways that could negatively affect their sense of agency and communion. By explicitly asking how the Sacred can be helpful or harmful, I hoped to develop space for Robert to safely voice distrust of the Church while helping him identify positive aspects of the Sacred in his life such as "honoring the Earth." Asking Cindy to reflect on Robert's story helped strengthen her agency while developing communion through witnessing his experience, making room for their spiritual differences, and expressing excitement about a shared relationship with the Sacred and their community.

Expand Upon Helpful, and Minimize Harmful, Experiences with the Sacred Based on my clinical experience with individuals and families struggling with chronic illnesses, I've found it is critical to expand upon helpful Sacred discourses while minimizing those that are harmful. During our fourth session, the couple reported spending time discussing their Sacred interests, and Robert contacted one of the elders in his community to update her about the couple's challenges with illness. I continued to highlight strengths and remain curious about how they could access resources using agency and communion skills:

Therapist: I'm pleasantly surprised, Robert. You've been reconnecting with your support system in your community. What's changed, and how were you able to do that?
Robert: Well, it wasn't too hard. I guess I felt embarrassed that I hadn't been in contact with them and I'd get the fifth degree. But I talked to Cindy and let her know how I felt and we decided it would be helpful for us to contact Julie and update her. I let Julie know why we haven't been in contact or involved and she was supportive of us.
Therapist: So, you and Cindy decided to open up a door that had been closed for a while. That's awesome. How did it feel to do that together Cindy?
Cindy: It felt good that Robert was willing to do something different for himself and for the both of us. We talked about taking back some control over our decisions rather than letting things happen and then not knowing how to get out of it. We agreed our Sacred beliefs are our top priority right now, right up there with our medical needs.
Therapist: So, the two of you have come to an agreement. If you decided to make another change, what would that look like and how would you move forward?
Cindy: I think I'd like to make specific plans to connect with our friends and families, so we don't feel isolated and get into a rut again. That includes attending Church, for me, and attending Native community events for both of us. At least on a weekly basis.
Therapist: Robert, how does connection to the Sacred help you move forward now?
Robert: I agree with you [looking at Cindy]. Putting it in our schedule like we do with our medical appointments will keep us committed and fill our cup and pay it forward.

By explicitly asking how the Sacred informs how they could move forward toward healing, I hoped to support their intentional decision to set boundaries around how and when to engage with the Sacred. As seen above, Robert was able to generate agency and invite helpful experiences of the Sacred in response to Cindy's bid for connection. This continued to make room for their spiritual differences while focusing on their shared relationship with the Sacred and their community.

Discussion and Clinical Implications

I recommend using the following guidelines for assessing, exploring, and expanding upon the Sacred as part of the BPSS Model.

Clinical Implications: The Integrative Process

Assess Assessing and gathering information about the Sacred during standard intake procedures and throughout the MedFT experience is critical for inclusive and responsive therapeutic processes. This focus honors the system's complex intersectional experiences. I've learned clients are in the expert position as teachers of their truth. As such, healthcare professionals such as MedFTs would benefit from placing themselves in a one-down position, as humble learners, using humility and sensitivity (Hoogestraat & Trammel, 2003) as well as developing carefully constructed questions that elicit powerful and authentic experiences.

Explore Similarly, MedFTs benefit greatly from intentionally creating the space to inquire about and explore the Sacred, reflect on beliefs, and gain awareness of how they influence choices and behaviors, particularly when working with both mental and physical health concerns. I've also learned that language is symbolic, and clients may respond favorably or adversely to certain terminology. Therefore, it is critical to remain flexible, listen, learn, and use words that resonate with rather than discount clients' and their families' Sacred experiences.

Expand Once the language and symbolism become explicit, MedFTs could expand upon Sacred experiences that affect health-related QOL by exploring abstract Sacred beliefs and values in more concrete ways. This helps clients identify empowering and oppressive beliefs and make positive changes within their systems.

Clinical Implications: Challenging Personal Processes

Over the years, I've learned to invest in a continuous Sacred self-assessment that includes a statement, a spiritual genogram, and an honest listing of my values, biases, triggers, strengths, and limitations (Hodge, 2005). Everyone has a belief system that permeates the therapeutic environment and directly affects the therapeutic relationship (see also Aponte, 2002). As MedFTs, our helpful and empowering beliefs encourage strengths and highlight advantages which mirror the systemic premise of couple and family therapy. This is why ongoing therapist training in the Sacred must include a rigorous self-reflective process which inherently can generate discomfort and anxiety. Social support, including supervision and consult groups, can be a valuable resource for therapists navigating such personal, self-reflective journeys.

Clinical Implications: Developing the Professional Processes

Being Direct Therapists can set the norm that the Sacred and its influence on functioning is an appropriate topic to broach in session and sends both an explicit and implicit message about the relevance of the Sacred in clients' lives.

Staying Systemic Simply talking about the Sacred with multiple individuals in session does not constitute systemic practice. The key is ensuring attention to the relational influences and processes, acknowledging similarities, and negotiating their differences.

Using Sacred Tools Therapists benefit from utilizing verbal and pictorial spiritual assessment tools such as those proposed by Hodge (2005) to expand the system's awareness of their Sacred experiences.

Attending to Power Power dynamics are often implicit and pervasive in Sacred systems. Inattention to power dynamics can cause inadvertent harm; thus, interventions in Sacred power dynamics counter potentially harmful power disparities within the system.

Consulting Sacred Leaders When integrating the Sacred, it may be beneficial to include clients' Sacred leaders to tease out difficult or misunderstood power dimensions. Seeking knowledge can provide therapists with insight into clients' worldviews.

Seeking Mentorship Supervision, mentorship, and personal therapy can significantly enhance professional skills and competence in integrating the Sacred. Staying connected to colleagues and seeking mentorship in any capacity reinforces ethical and legal best practices, enabling the navigation of clients' Sacred experiences with curiosity, humility, sensitivity, and care.

References

Aponte, H. (2002). Spirituality: The heart of therapy. *Journal of Family Psychotherapy, 13*(1/2), 13–27. https://doi.org/10.1300/J085v13n01_02

Engel, G. L. (1977). The need for a new medical model: A challenge for biomedicine. *Science, 196*(4286), 129–136. https://doi.org/10.1037/1091-7527.23.4.379

Esmiol Wilson, E. (2018). From assessment to activism: Utilizing a justice-informed framework to guide spiritual and religious clinical interventions. In E. Esmiol Wilson & L. A. Nice (Eds.), *Socially just religious and spiritual interventions: Ethical uses of therapeutic power, AFTA Springer Briefs*. Cham, Switzerland: Springer.

Hodge, D. R. (2005). Spiritual assessment in marital and family therapy: A methodological framework for selecting from among six qualitative assessment tools. *Journal of Marriage and Family Therapy, 31*(4), 341–356. https://doi.org/10.1111/j.1752-0606.2005.tb01575.x

Hodgson, J. L., Lamson, A., & Reese, L. (2007). The biopsychosocial-spiritual interview method. In D. Linville & K. M. Hertlein (Eds.), *The therapist's notebook for family health care: Homework, handouts, and activities for individuals, couples, and families coping with illness, loss, and disability* (pp. 3–12). New York: Haworth Press.

Hoogestraat, T., & Trammel, J. (2003). Spiritual and religious discussions in family therapy: Activities to promote dialogue. *The American Journal of Family Therapy, 31*(5), 413–426 https://doi.org/1080/01926180390224049

McDaniel, S. H., Doherty, W. J., & Hepworth, J. (Eds.). (2014). *Medical family therapy and integrated care* (2nd ed.). Washington, DC: American Psychological Association. https://doi.org/10.1002/anzf.1167

McDaniel, S. H., Hepworth, J., & Doherty, W. J. (Eds.). (1992). *Medical family therapy: A biopsychosocial approach to families with health problems*. New York: Basic Books.

Pruchno, R., Wilson-Genderson, M., & Cartwright, F. P. (2009). Depressive symptoms and marital satisfaction in the context of chronic disease: A longitudinal dyadic analysis. *Journal of Family Psychology, 23*(4), 573–584. https://doi.org/10.1037/a0015878

Ramirez, S. P., Macêdo, D. S., Sales, P. M., Figueiredo, S. M., Daher, E. F., Araújo, S. M., et al. (2012). The relationship between religious coping, psychological distress and quality of life in hemodialysis patients. *Journal of Psychosomatic Research, 72*, 129–135. https://doi.org/10.1016/j.jpsychores.2011.11.012

Timmers, L., Thong, M., Dekker, F. W., Boeschoten, E. W., Heijmans, M., Rijken, M., et al. (2008). Illness perceptions in dialysis patients and their association with quality of life. *Psychology & Health, 23*(6), 679–690. https://doi.org/10.1080/14768320701246535

Yong, D. S., Kwok, A. O., Wong, D. M., Suen, M. H., Chen, W. T., & Tse, D. M. (2009). Symptom burden and quality of life in end-stage renal disease: A study of 179 patients on dialysis and palliative care. *Palliative Medicine, 23*(2), 111–119. https://doi.org/10.1177/0269216308101099

Index

E. Esmiol Wilson, L. Nice (eds.), *Socially Just Religious and Spiritual Interventions*, AFTA SpringerBriefs in Family Therapy, https://doi.org/10.1007/978-3-030-01986-0

The manufacturer's authorised representative in the EU is Springer Nature Customer Service Centre GmbH, Europaplatz 3, 69115 Heidelberg, Germany. If you have any concerns regarding our products, please contact ProductSafety@springernature.com

Printed and bound by CPI Group (UK) Ltd, Croydon, CR0 4YY
30/09/2026
02225606-0018